Electronic Calculators

by

H. Edward Roberts

Edited by

Forrest M. Mims III

HOWARD W. SAMS & CO., INC.
THE BOBBS-MERRILL CO., INC.
INDIANAPOLIS • KANSAS CITY • NEW YORK

FIRST EDITION

SECOND PRINTING—1974

International Standard Book Number: 0-672-21039-8
Library of Congress Catalog Card Number: 74-75276

Preface

Thanks to the availability of economical electronic calculators, a lifetime of hand computations can now be condensed into a few hours. Calculators of all types are becoming more common than slide rules in university classes, businesses, and anywhere mathematical operations are performed, and it's safe to say that electronic calculators will make an important impact on society.

Although the electronics magazines have carried numerous articles on calculator design, fabrication, and component selection, until now none of this information has been compiled into book form. This book gathers together much of this information in a series of chapters on such topics as memories, displays, organization, interfacing, and servicing. The chapters on interfacing and servicing should be of particular interest since these two areas have received little treatment elsewhere.

Several individuals and firms have made important contributions to my own understanding of calculators and to this book. I am particularly indebted to Lawrence LeKashman, president of Olson Electronics, for his valuable advice concerning calculator marketing and his frequent encouragement. Lloyd McNeil of Hamilton-Avnet Electronics and Jack Pintar of Litronix have provided important advice regarding the selection of calculator components and displays. John Gates and Dan Fullerton of Hewlett-Packard provided information and photographs of their firm's calculator products. Jack Turk of MOS Technology also provided photomicrographs of calculator chips as well as other assistance.

Several of my employees at MITS, Inc. have also made valuable contributions to this book. Program Manager Patrick Godding wrote an article on servicing calculators for *Radio-Electronics* magazine from which Chapter 9 is adapted. Pat also helped write portions of Chapter 8 on calculator programmers. Director of Engineering Bill Yates has offered continued assistance and advice, and Elizabeth Dunlap, Director of Advertising, selected many of the photographs that appear in the book.

I am especially grateful for the assistance of my friend Forrest Mims. Besides coordinating and editing the manuscript, he wrote several of the chapters.

Finally, I am particularly indebted to my wife, Joan, for her understanding and patience. Her faithful encouragement and support made this book possible.

H. Edward Roberts

Contents

CHAPTER 6

CHAPTER 7

CHAPTER 8

CHAPTER 9

CHAPTER 10

CHAPTER 1

Evolution of the Electronic Calculator

Man's first counting machine was his two hands. Thus, it is no coincidence that the term *digit* refers to both the fingers and the numbers 0-10. Finger counting, which is actually primitive addition, is still used throughout the world. But even before recorded history, man invented counting techniques which permitted the counting of sums greater than the total of his fingers. Notched bones, marked sticks, and knotted strings made possible more advanced counting, an absolute requirement for timekeeping, bartering, and establishing formal commerce.

THE ABACUS

The earliest mechanical calculator was the abacus. It is believed that the abacus was in use in Egypt as early as 450 B.C., and a type of abacus may have been used in China as early as 600 B.C. The first abacuses consisted of small pebbles moved through grooves drawn in loose sand. The machine began to bear some resemblance to its modern form when the counting stones were placed in grooves formed in a wood or metal tablet.

The modern abacus (Fig. 1-1) consists of a frame which supports a dozen or more parallel rods. Five to seven movable beads or counters provide the counting mechanism. There is generally a central bar across the top center of the frame to separate one or two beads on each rod from the rest. The beads on top correspond to fives, while the counters below the dividing bar correspond to ones.

To place a number on an abacus, the frame is first cleared by moving all the one beads *down* and the five beads *up*. By assigning one rod to be the ones column and those to its left to be the tens, hundreds, and thousands columns, and so forth, it is easy to "write" numbers on the machine by moving the beads toward the central dividing bar.

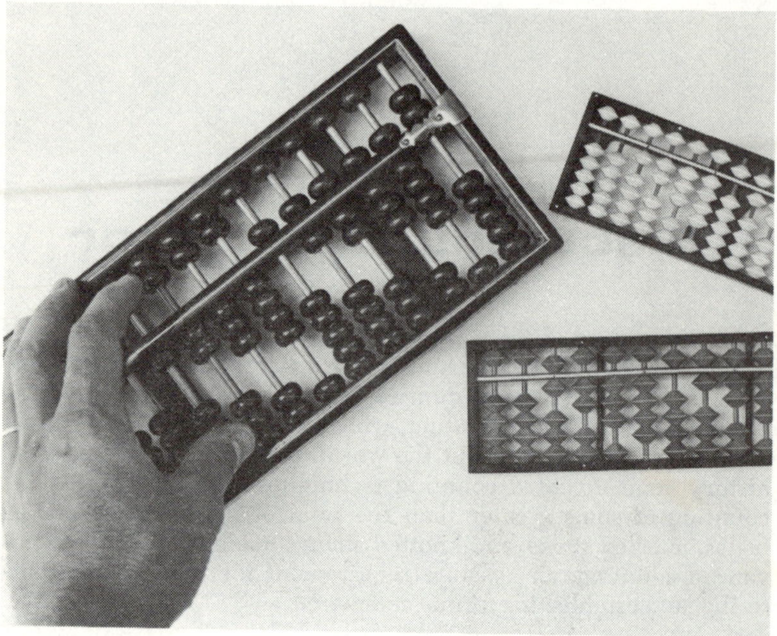

Fig. 1-1. Several Oriental abacuses.

Arithmetic with an abacus is remarkably simple and efficient, and with practice one can soon gain speed in the ancient art of abacus manipulation. In a now famous competition held in 1946 between a Japanese abacus operator and an American operator equipped with a mechanical adding machine, the abacus beat the calculator in four out of five areas of competition. The abacus was faster than the mechanical machine since the operator performs the arithmetic as new numbers are inserted into the machine. In the case of the desk calculator, the operator must activate a totaling mechanism before the final answer can be calculated, but the abacus provides a running total and the final answer is ready to read out as soon as the last number has been inserted onto the machine.

Abacuses are still in use throughout the Orient, the Soviet Union, and other parts of the world. Chinese-style abacuses have two beads on the top side and five on the bottom, while the modern Japanese version, the *soroban,* has one bead on top and four below. The soroban is designed for speed and efficiency since elimination of the additional beads forces the operator to "carry" as soon as each column of digits exceeds nine.

MECHANICAL ARITHMETIC

The abacus can easily be used for addition and subtraction by a beginner and for multiplication and division after a little practice. But as more advanced mathematical operations were developed, a need for more comprehensive calculating machines was created. The first significant step beyond the abacus was a gear-driven adding machine invented by Blaise Pascal in 1642. The teen-aged genius designed and assembled a mechanical calculator capable of adding series of eight-digit numbers. Fig. 1-2 shows a simple mechanical counter which is a modern descendent of Pascal's device. Another important 17th-Century invention was John Napier's device for calculating with logarithms, and still another was William Oughtred's invention of the slide rule. Fig. 1-3 shows a typical modern slide rule.

Fig. 1-2. Simple mechanical digital counter.

The basic concept of Pascal's mechanical adder is found in modern mechanical adding machines (Fig. 1-4), and slide rules are still an important tool of modern engineering. But no inventor foresaw the evolution of the modern calculator as clearly as Charles Babbage.

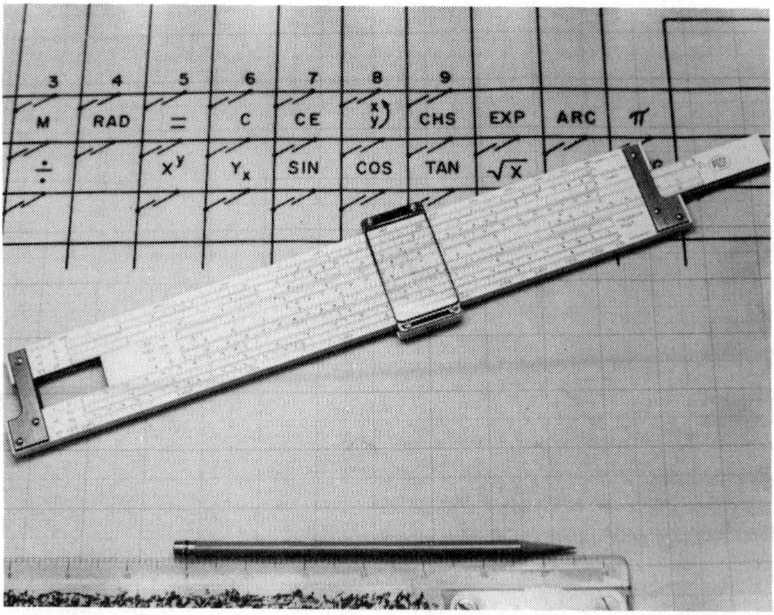

Fig. 1-3. Engineering slide rule.

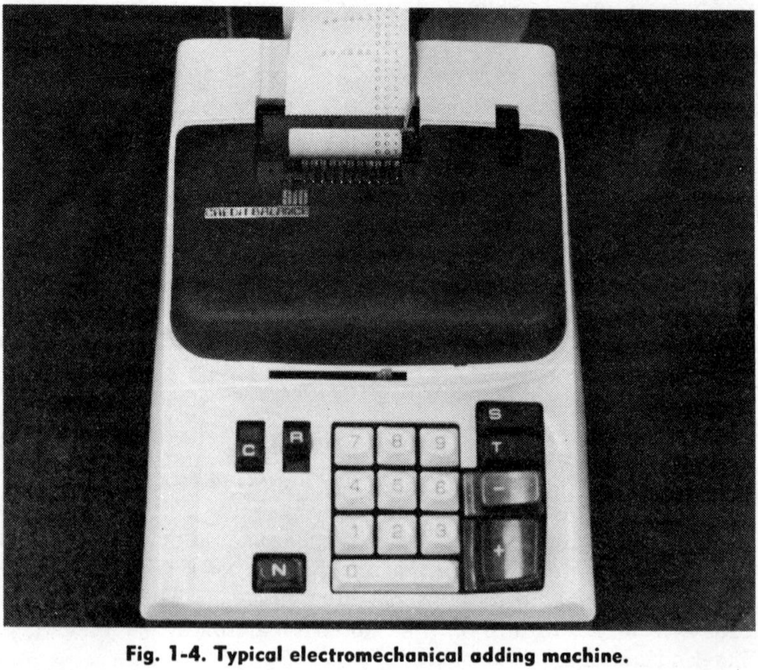

Fig. 1-4. Typical electromechanical adding machine.

THE ANALYTICAL ENGINE

Babbage, an outspoken mathematician and philosopher, was obsessed with the idea of designing and constructing an advanced mechanical calculator which would perform the four basic arithmetic functions as well as advanced manipulations of these fundamental operations.

In 1822 Babbage succeeded in constructing the "Difference Engine" for the solution of polynomial equations ($x^2 + x + a = 0$). The success of the machine convinced him that he could construct a more advanced calculator, the Analytical Engine, having punched-card input, a memory of one thousand 50-digit numbers, and both visual and hard-copy output.

Unfortunately in Babbage's time machining processes were not sufficiently advanced to permit all the required mechanical parts of his highly complex Analytical Engine to be constructed with the necessary degree of precision. The apparatus required hundreds of precision mechanical components. Though Babbage completed literally thousands of intricate engineering drawings detailing the assembly and the internal operation of the machine, a feat in itself, the precision tooling required for fabricating the working parts was just not available.

Babbage spent the last 40 years of his life working on the Analytical Engine and died in 1841 without seeing his project completed. He did, however, make important contributions to the science of machining, and he designed the basic organization of a modern digital computer system. Indeed, some of the operations which would have been performed on Babbage's Analytical Engine bear an amazing resemblance to some of the basic FORTRAN statements used with many modern computers.

DIGITAL AND ANALOG ARITHMETIC

By the beginning of the 20th Century, the basics of the two major classes of calculating machines had been discovered. The digital calculator, as represented by the abacus and other primitive counting systems, had reached its pinnacle with Babbage's Analytical Engine. And slide rules and Lord Kelvin's tide prediction machine, an 1872 invention, represented the analog calculators. While both digital and analog calculators were designed to perform arithmetic and even differential equations in the case of Kelvin's machine, their operation was fundamentally different.

Digital calculators utilize discrete quantities in making calculations, while analog calculators solve problems by substituting a mechanical or electrical analogy of the physical quantities being calculated. The differences between the two types of calculators give each relative advantages and disadvantages. Digital machines, for example, are far more accurate than their analog counterparts, and large-capacity digital devices can express answers accurate to better than one part in a trillion.

Modern digital calculators are limited in accuracy mainly by the number of readout elements. For example, a machine with a 14-digit display has an *output* accuracy of one part in 10^{14}, while potential accuracy is much higher. The accuracy of an analog device will rarely exceed 0.01%.

Analog calculators do have advantages, however, and they are well suited for modeling solutions for a variety of conditions. In aerodynamics, for example, analog calculators and computers are frequently used to simulate aircraft shapes. By simply turning potentiometers connected to simulate drag, velocity, air density, and other parameters, it is possible to conveniently select optimum aircraft configurations for particular flight requirements.

ELECTRONIC COMPUTERS

Getting back to the evolution of calculators, there were a number of important developments at the turn of the century which directly affected future prospects for both analog and digital cal-

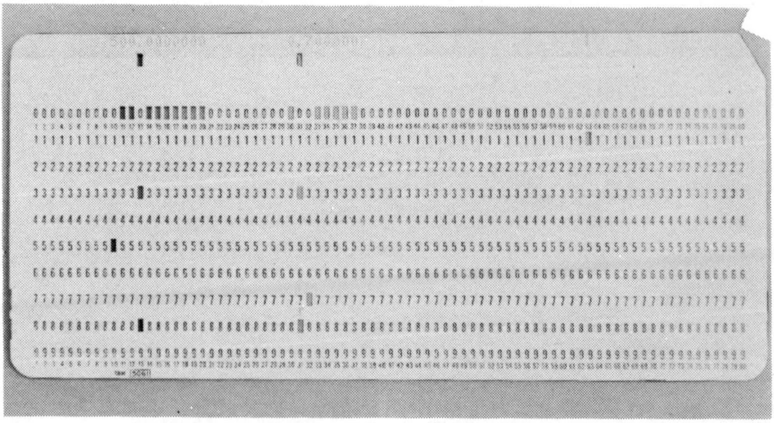

Fig. 1-5. An IBM card.

culating machines. One of the most important of these was the invention by Dr. Herman Hollerith of electrically read punched cards. The Hollerith cards were first developed for use in the United States census of 1890, and they are direct predecessors of the modern IBM card (Fig. 1-5).

The next big advance in the calculator field was the development in 1925 of a large analog computer by Dr. Vannevar Bush. An advanced version of the Bush machine was secretly used during World War II to calculate artillery-firing tables. Also in World War II, a complex analog calculating system was used in the fire-control system of B-29 bombers.

In 1944 interest in calculating machines suddenly shifted from analog devices back to digital techniques with the completion of the Mark I Automatic Sequence Controlled Calculator. Containing more than 3000 relays, the Mark I could multiply two 23-digit numbers, its maximum capacity, in 4½ seconds. The Mark I was conceived by Howard Aiken and built with the assistance of IBM. While designing the calculator, Aiken came upon some of Babbage's work and recognized its contribution to the principles of complex digital calculating machines. Aiken once remarked, "If Babbage had lived 75 years later, I would have been out of a job."

The Mark I was followed by an even more significant calculating machine. In 1946 Drs. J. Presper Eckert and John Mauchly completed the ENIAC (Electronic Numerical Integrator and Calculator), a significant advance over the Mark I in that it used high-speed vacuum tubes instead of the much slower electromechanical relays. The new machine was a major scientific and engineering accomplishment, but it presented some major problems as well. With 18,000 tubes, 11,000 switches and terminals, and more than a half-million solder connections, the ENIAC required two and one-half years to assemble and more than 1800 square feet of floor space. But the added complexity gave the ENIAC much faster speed than the Mark I. While the relay machine required one-third of a second to add two numbers, the ENIAC could perform 5000 additions in one second.

The ENIAC marked the beginning of the computer age, and it was soon followed by high-capacity machines, such as the EDSAC (Electronic Delay Storage Automatic Calculator), EDVAC (Electronic Discrete Variable Automatic Calculator), and SSEC (Selective Sequence Electronic Calculator). The EDSAC was unique in that it incorporated a *stored program* for the first time.

The stored program, a key to the success of modern digital calculators and computers, provides the internal instructions necessary for a calculator or computer to perform complex operations with a minimum of outside instructions. A typical stored program, for example, will provide the necessary instructions for determining trigonometric functions. The operator is then saved the laborious task of encoding the appropriate instructions each time he needs to refer to such a function. In a typical operation, he merely instructs the machine to find the cosine (or tangent, or sine) of a particular angle, and with a few code letters (usually "COS" in the case of cosine), the internally stored program of the machine automatically furnishes the arithmetic section with the detailed instructions required for the operation. Large digital computers frequently use magnetic tape for stored programs, while advanced electronic desk calculators employ solid-state memories for the same purpose.

In 1951 Eckert and Mauchly completed work on the famous UNIVAC, the first modern digital computer. The original version of this machine was purchased by the United States Census Bureau and was used until 1963 when it was replaced by more modern equipment. The first UNIVAC is now on permanent exhibition, along with several other pioneering calculating devices, at the Smithsonian Institution in Washington, D.C.

During the 1950's the UNIVAC was followed by a series of advanced digital computers developed by the computer industry.

SEMICONDUCTOR ELECTRONICS

Although the transistor had been invented in 1948, most computers employed vacuum tubes. But in the late fifties and early sixties, reliability of the machines was significantly enhanced when the switch to transistor operation was accomplished. In addition to improving reliability, the use of transistors meant that the once-bulky computers could be squeezed into much smaller spaces. Fig. 1-6 compares a typical vacuum tube with a few typical transistors. The size reductions were vital to military and civilian aerospace endeavors since, for the first time, it became possible for an aircraft or missile to carry along its own portable digital computer for inertial navigation and other important roles. These early avionics computers were primitive by present-day standards, but they represented an enormous step forward at the time of their introduction.

The semiconductor developments which made possible compact digital-computer systems led to speculation about the prospects for electronic desk calculators. Integrated circuits (ICs) had been invented by Texas Instruments in the late 1950's, and major technological improvements by Fairchild a few years later made possible the formation of several dozen electronic components on a single silicon substrate. Fig. 1-7 shows a typical IC and the parts it replaces. Since even the first ICs crammed tens of components into the space normally required for one, and since the components were all connected together within the IC itself, for the first time it became feasible to consider designing electronic desk calculators.

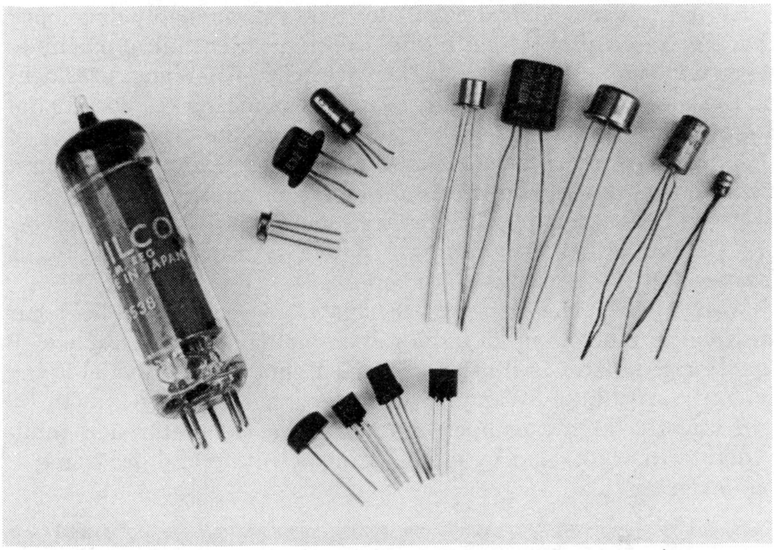

Fig. 1-6. Vacuum tube and several typical transistors.

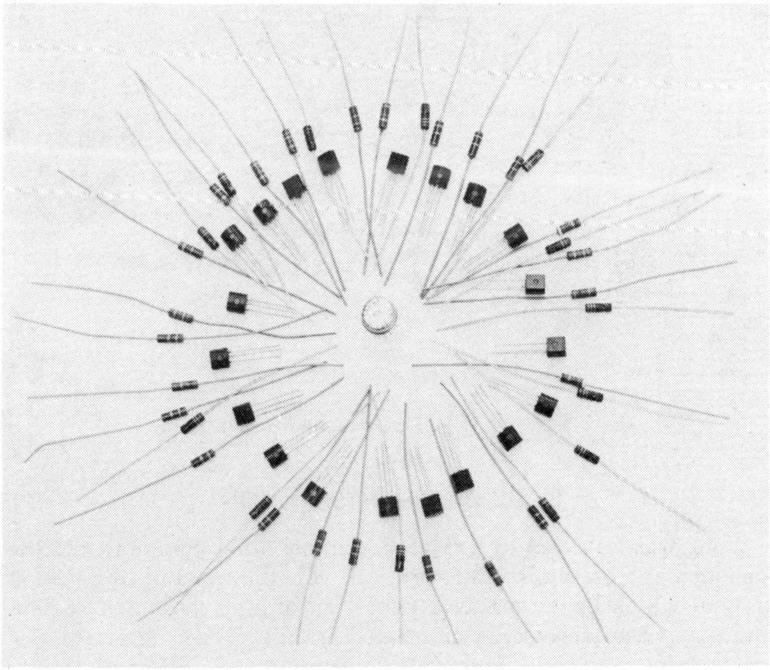

Fig. 1-7. Typical bipolar integrated circuit and the components it replaces.

At first, the mechanical-calculator field was so highly developed that electronic alternatives to the traditional mechanical machines were noncompetitive. In 1964, however, Dr. An Wang, president of the electronics firm which bears his name, devised a digital logarithmic converter which made possible the development of practical and competitive electronic desk calculators for the first time. Wang, one of the inventors of the magnetic core memory, founded his company in 1951 after leaving the Harvard University Computational Laboratory. A native of China, he came to the United States as a graduate student in 1945.

Wang's early leadership in the electronic calculator field has resulted in more than 25 basic calculator models, some of which are described later in this book. Fig. 1-8 shows a late-model Wang scientific calculator. Wang's firm has managed steady growth by avoiding the highly competitive miniature calculator and minicomputer markets and by emphasizing scientific and programmable machines.

Courtesy Wang

Fig. 1-8. Wang 452 advanced scientific calculator.

LARGE-SCALE INTEGRATION

Wang was followed by Friden and a few other companies in the development of semiconductor desk calculators, but the development which began a literal explosion of electronic desk calculators was the large-scale integrated circuit (LSI). A product of metal-oxide semiconductor (MOS) technology, LSI made possible the compression of the hundreds, and even thousands, of tran-

Fig. 1-9. Photomicrograph of typical MOS LSI calculator chip.

sistors and other components required to perform the computer operations of arithmetic, memory, and control onto several semiconductor "chips," each about a tenth of an inch square. Fig. 1-9 is a photomicrograph of a typical MOS LSI calculator chip, and Fig. 1-10 shows a calculator chip installed in its mounting package. With the availability of calculator chips, it became feasible to manufacture multiple-function electronic desk calculators that required less space than a telephone.

A size comparison between a modern LSI calculator and the first vacuum-tube calculator, the ENIAC, is truly impressive. The ENIAC required an entire room to house its racks of 18,000 vacuum tubes; a miniature LSI calculator, containing the equivalent of 30,000 transistors, will easily slip into a shirt pocket.

Continued developments in LSI technology have dramatically improved electronic calculators. Now, for example, nearly all the electronics required for a basic four-function calculator (+, −, ×,

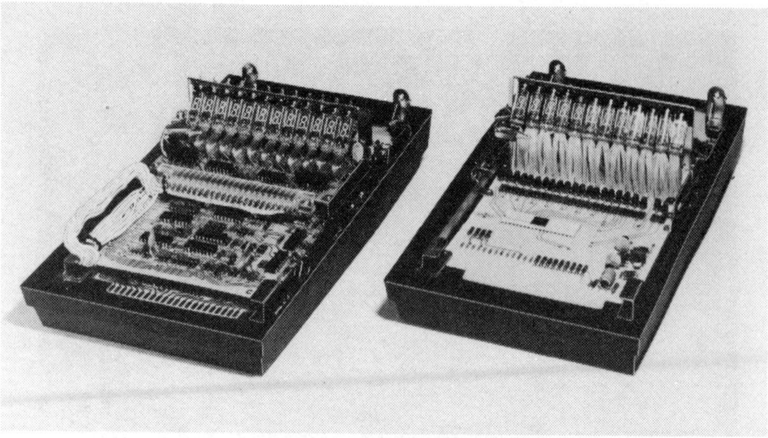

Fig. 1-10. Calculator chip package.

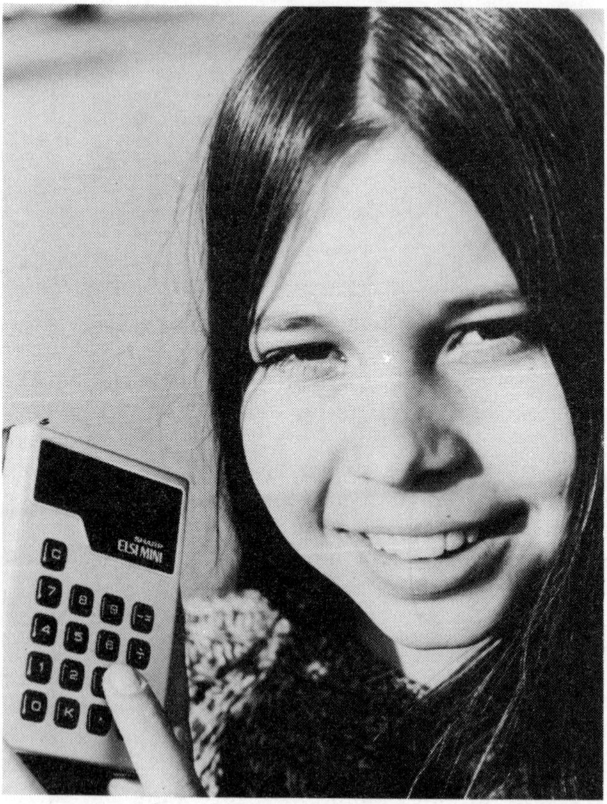

Fig. 1-11. Sharp ELSI MINI miniature four-function calculator.

÷) can be placed on a single LSI chip. The result is a calculator no larger than a portable transistor radio (Fig. 1-11). In addition to LSI, these new calculators employ such recent developments as light emitting diode (LED) displays and thermal printers. The market is highly competitive, and more than a dozen firms produce the miniature machines.

METAL-OXIDE SEMICONDUCTORS

The heart of most calculator chips is the metal-oxide-semiconductor (MOS) transistor. The basic MOS transistor can have one of two polarities. The p-channel (PMOS) devices consist of a slab of p-type silicon upon which two n-type regions have been formed. The n-type regions are called the *source* and *drain* and are separated by what is termed a *channel.* A very thin layer of insulating oxide is deposited over the channel, and a metal electrode called the *gate* is affixed to the oxide directly over the channel. Fig. 1-12 shows the construction of a simplified MOS transistor.

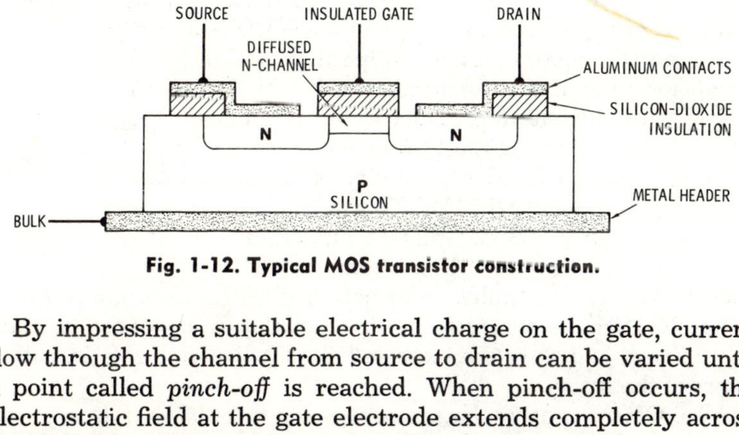

Fig. 1-12. Typical MOS transistor construction.

By impressing a suitable electrical charge on the gate, current flow through the channel from source to drain can be varied until a point called *pinch-off* is reached. When pinch-off occurs, the electrostatic field at the gate electrode extends completely across the channel and current flow is halted.

Due to the insulating layer between the gate and the channel of an MOS transistor, input impedance to the device is extremely high. For this reason, MOS transistors require far less operating current than their conventional bipolar transistor counterparts.

Thus far we have described only the PMOS transistor, but there are dozens of variations in this exceptionally versatile family of semiconductors. The NMOS, as the acronym implies, is the complement of PMOS. Instead of a p channel, an n substrate is employed to give an n-type channel. Likewise, the source and drain are of p-type material.

By incorporating an additional diffusion process in a silicon chip, both p- and n-type MOS structures can be formed on a single substrate. The result is a complementary MOS (CMOS). The CMOS results in even less power dissipation than either the PMOS or the NMOS. For example, a typical PMOS or NMOS transistor requires from 0.5 to 2.0 microwatts during operation. While this is a miniscule power requirement, particularly when compared to conventional bipolar devices, CMOS reduces power dissipation to practically nothing. The result is a boon to battery-operated portable equipment, such as electronic watches and pocket calculators. Converting these generalities to numbers, a CMOS circuit will consume only nanowatts in a standby mode and microwatts in the operational mode. Faster speeds (e.g., greater than 100 kHz) require more power.

The PMOS is the key to almost all conventional calculator chips. The CMOS has certain operating advantages over the MOS, but lacks the component density of the less complex PMOS. Additionally, the CMOS is more difficult to fabricate, since both PMOS and NMOS structures must be made on the same substrate. For this reason, the CMOS involves a more expensive manufacturing process than either the PMOS or the NMOS.

Currently, most calculator chips incorporate PMOS logic and memories. Only a limited number of calculator memory chips use NMOS, but this situation is expected to change in coming years with NMOS becoming the leading contender in LSI technology.

An example of NMOS capability is Motorola's 8192-bit NMOS read-only memory (ROM). This advanced ROM contains 128 high-resolution 7×9 dot matrix alphanumeric characters. This device is compatible with conventional TTL logic and can be used to generate complex information displays on a CRT. Additional NMOS memories are being developed by Motorola and other firms, and they are expected to play a major role in calculators of the future.

Also, CMOS may make inroads in the calculator industry. Although packing densities are not nearly so great as NMOS and PMOS, CMOS offers the potential of random-access memories (RAMs) with very low standby power. The result would be a calculator with a nonvolatile RAM, since a tiny trickle of continuous current would preserve the contents of the memory. Such a development would significantly enhance the capability of many multifunction calculators.

While MOS circuitry has made possible the LSI revolution, it is not without disadvantage. The major problem with MOS chips is a direct result of the oxide film which permits their field effect action. The oxide film is impervious to normal operating voltages, but a tiny amount of static electricity packs enough potential to easily penetrate the oxide. The result is a short from gate to channel and a circuit failure.

The static electricity problem with MOS devices is so great that special shipping, packaging, and installation procedures must be used. The MOS field-effect transistors are shipped with their leads twisted together, and MOS integrated circuits are packaged in conductive envelopes or on foil-covered foamed plastic blocks. Even the static electricity generated during circuit assembly or stray voltage from a soldering iron can damage a MOS device, so sockets are invariably used and MOS devices are installed only when the circuit is completely assembled.

PMOS VERSUS NMOS

Fundamental differences in manufacturing give NMOS at least a 15% greater packaging density over PMOS. Its higher density, coupled with nearly 50% faster speed and lower voltage requirement, gives NMOS a significant advantage over the current PMOS.

PMOS is still the predominant calculator-chip technology, but NMOS random-access memories are expected to be introduced by many major semiconductor manufacturers.

What significance will NMOS have for electronic calculators? Simple four-function machines will have no need for the improvements in density and speed offered by NMOS. Programmable machines, however, will benefit greatly from the availability of 4096-bit random-access memories which are fully TTL compatible.

MINIATURE ELECTRONIC CALCULATORS

Most miniature calculators employ LED or electrofluorescent displays, but a few units incorporate liquid-crystal displays or paper-tape printouts. Most pocket calculators are limited to the four basic arithmetic functions and storage of a constant, but improvements in MOS LSI technology have recently permitted more functions to be included. A few pocket machines have extra capabilities, such as user-accessible memory, trigonometric functions, logarithms, square and square root capabilities, and U.S. standard numbering to metric conversions. Many of these functions can be achieved with single key strokes. Miniature calculators will continue to incorporate additional functions in the future. In fact, keyboard space, which cannot be reduced beyond practical operating limits, will be the only limiting factor. Already several machines incorporate a special *shift* key which automatically changes the function of a select group of keys and greatly increases calculating power.

Miniature calculators are popular with students and anyone else on the go who requires math assistance. For desk operation, machines about the size of a cigar box are standard. Dozens of different types from as many manufacturers are now available. The prospective purchaser can choose from units that include such added features as memory capability, printers (electronic and electromechanical), special functions, and novel keyboard manipulation shortcuts.

Prices for miniature and desk calculators begin at just under $50 and range up to several thousand dollars for a machine equipped with a printer and peripheral equipment. As with any other purchase, the buyer gets what he pays for, and the cheaper machines do not necessarily represent the best bargain. Many of the low-cost machines require special keyboard manipulations to perform simple problems in addition and subtraction.

KIT CALCULATORS

A possible solution for the prospective purchaser with a limited budget and some soldering iron experience is one of the new kit calculators. Micro Instrumentation and Telemetry Systems, Inc. (MITS) has been selling kit desk calculators since 1971 and now offers a line of machines ranging from a miniature machine to a full-function scientific calculator. Fig. 1-13 shows a MITS Model 1440 desk calculator, a kit machine incorporating memory and

Courtesy MITS

Fig. 1-13. MITS 1440 multiple-function kit calculator.

Fig. 1-14. MITS 941 Metric Converter multiple-function calculator.

Courtesy MITS

square-root functions. The MITS Model 941, an advanced miniature calculator having 41 separate functions, is shown in Fig. 1-14.

Heathkit brought out a kit calculator in 1972 and now offers both pocket and desk models.

Prices for kit calculators are low. For example, MITS offers a four-function machine with a six-digit readout for less than $50. An assembled version of the same machine can be purchased for an additional $10.

Kit calculators are not difficult to assemble. Besides saving money, assembly of a kit machine provides background for future troubleshooting and enhances the kit builder's knowledge of general calculator construction and operation. Fig. 1-15 shows the parts supplied with a typical machine. The instructions manuals provided by both Heath and MITS are so clearly presented that even persons with little or no kit-building experience can successfully assemble a complete calculator.

SCIENTIFIC CALCULATORS

The development of other specialized calculator chips, particularly memories, has further enhanced calculator performance, and now several companies are marketing *scientific* calculators. These

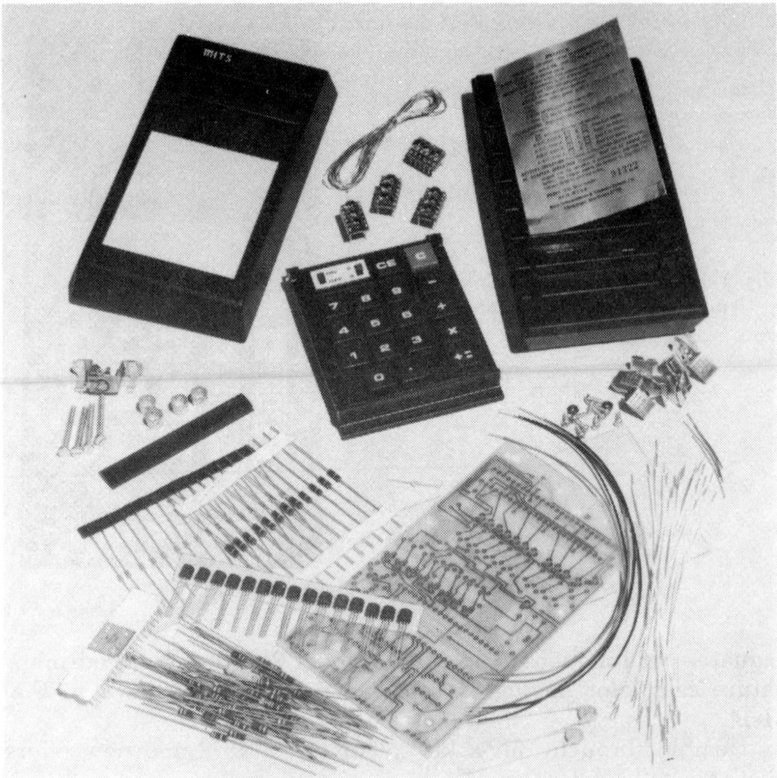

Courtesy MITS

Fig. 1-15. Components supplied with typical kit calculator (MITS 1200).

machines include the standard four arithmetic functions on their keyboards but supplement the basic capability with keys for the various trigonometric functions, pi, square and square root, e^x, logarithms, and other operations common to mathematics. In this way, the scientific calculator becomes an instantly accessible book of mathematical tables as well as an easily operated calculating machine. Fig. 1-16 shows a miniature scientific calculator, the Hewlett-Packard HP-35.

The scientific calculator has the ability to perform complex operations as a result of the same kind of internally stored program used in large-scale computers. Read-only-memory (ROM) chips store the microinstructions necessary to tell the calculator arithmetic unit to calculate the desired mathematical function. Since the expanded capability of the scientific machines is largely dependent on the capacity of the ROM, it is possible to further ex-

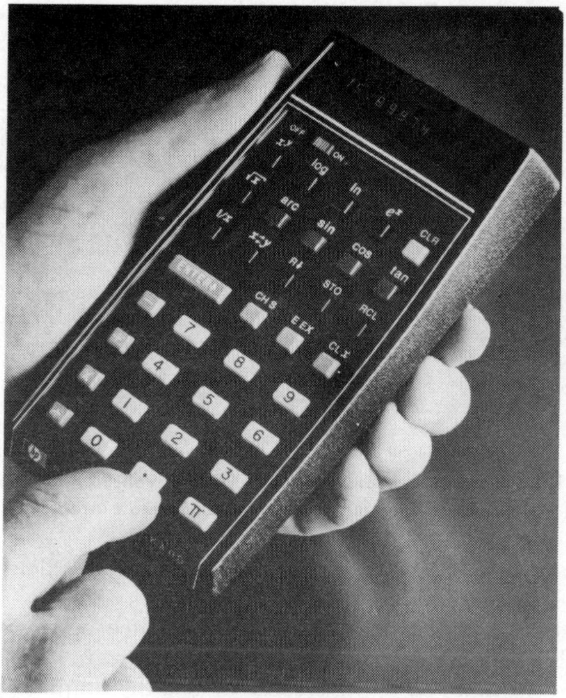

Courtesy Hewlett-Packard

Fig. 1-16. Hewlett-Packard HP-35 miniature scientific calculator.

pand an existing machine by merely adding plug-in memory modules. Several manufacturers offer scientific calculators compatible with a variety of memory modules which literally let the operator custom-design his own keyboard in the time it takes to insert the module into the machine. A bank of unmarked keys is used to specify the operations and functions contained within the special ROM modules, and a snap-in label card notes the newly assigned function of each key. The calculator can be "redesigned" in the time it takes to exchange the ROM modules.

PROGRAMMABLE CALCULATORS

In what has become one of the fastest moving fields in electronics technology in recent years, scientific calculators have led to the next logical development—the programmable calculator. With the operating ease of a calculator and the power of a small computer, programmable calculators fill an important gap between scientific calculators and minicomputers. Fig. 1-17 shows

Courtesy Hewlett-Packard

Fig. 1-17. Hewlett-Packard 9810 and 9820 advanced programmable calculators (partially disassembled to show interior).

an interior view of two advanced programmable calculators, the Hewlett-Packard HP-9810 and 9820.

It is important to understand the difference between the programmable calculator and the minicomputer. In the important area of operational ease, the calculator has the unquestioned lead. Programmable calculators with an algebraic keyboard can handle complex equations just as they are written on paper, while a computer program must be written before the minicomputer will handle similar problems.

The approachability of a programmable calculator over a minicomputer is best illustrated by a typical problem-solving procedure. To determine the sine of an angle with a FORTRAN language minicomputer, for example, the machine must be given a set of specific instructions and the angle, usually by means of a typewriter-style keyboard. Fig. 1-18 shows a typical computer terminal used to address a computer from a remote location. The same problem can be solved on a calculator by merely keying-in the angle (unless it is already in the display) and pressing the SIN key. Obviously, the calculator solution is far easier and faster to implement.

Cost is another important area where the calculator comes out ahead. Programmable calculators can be purchased for about $3000, and $10,000 will buy a fully expanded model with accessories such as additional memory, printer, plotter, and input devices. The price may seem high to the uninitiated, but for the calculating power it's a genuine bargain.

Courtesy IBM

Fig. 1-18. IBM 3670 stock terminal.

For those who cannot afford the price of a programmable machine but are eager to have one anyway, help has arrived in the form of a kit programming unit. MITS, Inc. has introduced a programmer kit which can be mated to its machines already on the market. The cost for a complete kit programming unit and calculator will be about one-tenth that of a correspondingly assembled unit. A MITS 7440 series scientific calculator and programmer will provide the technician, engineer, or experimenter with many of the capabilities of a minicomputer.

So there you have it. The primitive abacus, a 3000-year old digital calculator still being used throughout the world, has finally been outclassed by electronics. In a development which would have been labeled as science fiction just ten years ago, complete programmable calculating systems which fit on a standard desk top and multiple-function machines which fit in a shirt pocket are available today.

CHAPTER 2

Electronic Arithmetic

The large-scale availability of economical electronic calculators has stimulated a revived interest in electronic arithmetic. This chapter will describe how a series of keyboard entries is changed into a solution by means of the binary number system. The binary system will be explained, and several fundamental binary logic and counting circuits will be presented.

THE BINARY SYSTEM

The use of binary or two-digit number schemes for control and arithmetic operations is not new. The early player piano is an excellent example of how a simple on/off code, i.e., absence or presence of a hole in a paper scroll, can be used to control a relatively complex instrument. The simplest electronic circuit that gives a two-position code is the on-off switch. The logic functions of the basic mechanical on-off switch can be implemented in an automated fashion by means of conducting or nonconducting transistors, relays, SCRs, FETs, and other components.

While the binary system is basically simple, most people find it awkward at first since they have been conditioned to count with the traditional base 10 or decimal system. In order to design and use binary logic, it is important to understand the binary numbering system. Fortunately, the system is relatively easy to understand if a few basic rules are remembered.

In any number system, the position of a digit determines its significance as well as the digit value. Consider, for example, the number 732:

$$732 = (7 \times 10^2) + (3 \times 10^1) + (2 \times 10^0)$$

This breakdown of a number shows that the position of each digit determines which power of ten the digit is to be multiplied by. For readers a little rusty in math, a number raised to the 0 power equals 1 (e.g., $10^0 = 1$; $2^0 = 1$; etc.). Also, any number raised to the 1 power equals itself (e.g., $10^1 = 10$; $2^1 = 2$; etc.). The binary system has the same position characteristics as the decimal system, except the multiplier is a power of 2 instead of 10. Also, the binary system allows only two digits: 0 and 1.

The following example shows the composition of a typical binary number:

$$\begin{aligned} 1001_2 &= [(1 \times 2^3) + (0 \times 2^2) + (0 \times 2^1) + (1 \times 2^0)]_{10} \\ &= [8 + 0 + 0 + 1]_{10} \\ &= 9_{10} \end{aligned}$$

NOTE: Subscript $_2$ denotes binary system, while subscript $_{10}$ denotes decimal system.

The previous example shows that a base 2 binary number can be analyzed in the same manner as a base 10 decimal number. In the binary system, the place multiplier is always a power of 2, while in the decimal system the multiplier is always a power of 10. The primary difference between the two systems, of course, is the binary system has only two digits and the decimal has ten. If these fundamental exceptions are followed, the binary system can be implemented by following the rules of the decimal system.

You can test your understanding of binary numbers by performing the above operation for several binary numbers. In addition to improving one's understanding of binary arithmetic, the technique is handy for converting binary to decimal notation.

The following table has the binary numbers for 0 through 9 already worked out:

Decimal (Base 10)	*Binary (Base 2)*
0	0000
1	0001
2	0010
3	0011
4	0100
5	0101
6	0110
7	0111
8	1000
9	1001

The four-digit binary numbers shown in the table have an important significance in calculator operation. They are called *binary-coded decimal* (bcd). The significance of bcd is that all ten decimal digits can be represented by a four-digit binary code.

Now that binary numbering has been explained, let's discuss binary arithmetic. Binary addition is performed in a similar manner to decimal addition. The only difference is that a carry occurs if the sum of two binary digits is greater than 1. The following examples demonstrate this principle:

$$\text{(a)}\quad \begin{array}{r} 1 \\ +\;\; \\ 1 \\ \hline 10_2 = 2_{10} \end{array}$$

In the decimal system, $1 + 1 = 2$, but the digit 2 is not allowed in the binary system. Therefore, when a binary operation gives a result greater than 1, the answer must be carried to the next column. In the case of adding two binary 1's, the result is greater than 1. Therefore, a 1 is carried to the next column and a 0 placed in the first colmun. This gives 10_2, which is the correct result.

Another example illustrates the carry operation:

$$\text{(b)}\quad \begin{array}{r} 10 \\ +\;\; \\ 10 \\ \\ 101 \\ \hline 1001_2 = 9_{10} \end{array}$$

As in example (a), note how a result exceeding binary 1 is carried to the next column. The addition procedure can be simplified by determining the number of pairs of 1's and placing a 1 in the next column for each pair. The carrying process is continued until all excess 1's are eliminated.

Two more examples will be provided to illustrate the carrying process. The reader should check the results by means of the method described above.

$$\text{(c)}\quad \begin{array}{r} 11 \\ +\;\; \\ 11 \\ \hline 110_2 = 6_{10} \end{array} \qquad\qquad \text{(d)}\quad \begin{array}{r} 1011 \\ +\;\; \\ 1101 \\ \hline 11000_2 = 24_{10} \end{array}$$

To gain a better understanding of binary addition, try several other examples and check the results by converting to the decimal system and adding. Binary subtraction employs similar techniques, and in most computing circuits, subtraction is performed by *complementary* addition. Multiplication is normally performed by repetitive addition and division by repetitive subtraction. The result of these operations is highly significant since all four arithmetic operations can be performed with a binary adder circuit.

Binary calculations may seem slow when accomplished by hand, and repetitive addition and subtraction to accomplish multiplication and division may seem inefficient. But electronic counting circuits are so fast, that binary operations are performed quite rapidly. For example, a typical calculator such as the MITS 1440 can add two 56-digit binary numbers in less than 1 millisecond and can multiply the same numbers in approximately 180 milliseconds. The MITS 7440 scientific calculator is even faster and can add two 76-bit binary numbers in approximately 130 microseconds.

LOGIC CIRCUITS

In addition to performing arithmetic operation, a calculator or computer must be capable of making logical decisions based on certain data. Even the performance of arithmetic operations requires a considerable number of automatic, internal logic decisions.

These logic decisions are made by electronic *logic circuits.* The circuits normally maintain one of two states (0 or 1) on their output. The output state is determined by the existence of certain specific requirements at the logic circuit input. For example, an AND gate circuit will produce an output signal only if *all* the inputs (there may be two or more) are at the correct state. An OR gate circuit will produce an output if *any* of its inputs are at the correct state.

A special terminology has been generated to explain the operation of logic circuits. A logic circuit can accept or generate only two basic states, and these are frequently called *true* and *false* conditions. In *positive logic,* a true condition is defined as a binary 1 and a false condition as binary 0. A binary 1 is represented electrically by the most positive voltage present, while a binary 0 is represented by the lowest voltage.

In practical transistor-transistor logic (TTL), a 1 or true state is represented by a voltage greater than approximately 3 volts, while a 0 or false state is represented by a voltage of less than 0.6 volts. Some logic systems employ *negative logic* wherein the voltage states are opposite those given above. Positive logic is employed throughout this book.

An important practical example of the need for logic circuits in a calculator is the generation of a seven-segment readout format for the display. Since the calculator performs arithmetic operations in a BCD (binary-coded decimal) mode, the output could simply consist of a row of lamps which indicated the output register content of the calculator in binary. All activated lamps would correspond to 1, while unactivated lamps would correspond to 0. As we have already noted, however, binary is a cumbersome system, and it is very convenient to have a digital output wherein the calculator output is displayed numerically in decimal numbers.

It is possible to convert a BCD signal into a seven-segment digital format with an array of logic gates. The operation is complex, and some 70 separate gates are required. Fortunately for the logic designer, seven-segment decoders are available as single integrated circuits from many semiconductor manufacturers. There are many other cases where single ICs are available for complex logic operations, but there are also many cases where the logic designer must build up circuits with individual gates.

Before describing the various types of logic in more detail, a few words on symbology are in order. Until very recently, literally dozens of logic symbol systems were in use. Fortunately a standard set of symbols has been developed and it is known as MIL-SPEC 801B. These standard symbols are now used by most semiconductor manufacturers, and they are used in this book.

AND Gates

The AND gate is a circuit which requires a 1 signal on all of its inputs to give a 1 signal at the output. Any other condition will produce a 0 on the output. Normally, 1 is represented by a high-voltage state, while 0 is represented by a low or zero voltage. Fig. 2-1 shows the standard logic symbol for an AND gate.

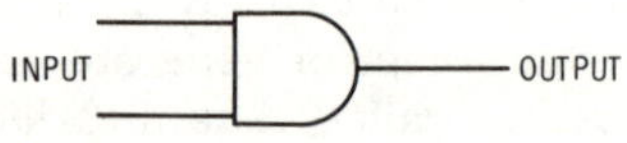

Fig. 2-1. Symbol for AND gate.

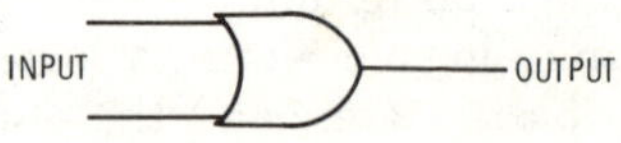

Fig. 2-2. Symbol for OR gate.

OR Gates

The OR gate will produce a 1 on its output when a 1 appears on any of its inputs. If no 1 is present at the input, the output will always be 0. The standard logic symbol for an OR gate is shown in Fig. 2-2.

NOT Circuits

A NOT circuit is simply an inverter that complements the input signal. Since there are only two binary states, it follows that a

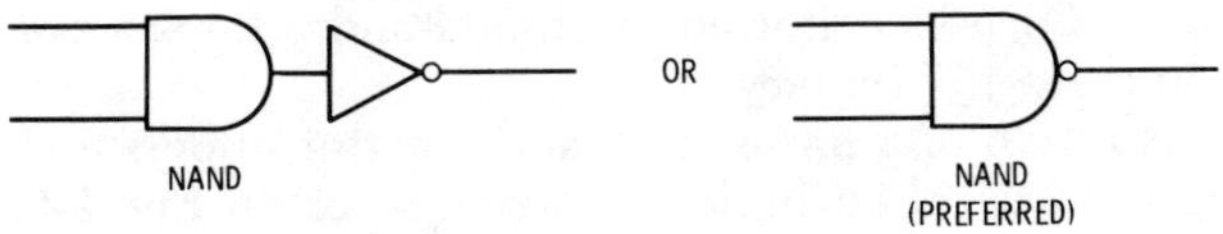

Fig. 2-3. Symbol for NAND gate.

NOT 1 is a 0 and vice versa. The NOT circuit is represented as a triangle and a small circle.

NAND and NOR Gates

In practice the most common logic circuits are NAND and NOR gates. These circuits are simply AND and OR gates followed by an inverter (NOT circuit) on the output. The symbols for NAND and NOR gates are shown in Figs. 2-3 and 2-4. Note the symbol for the NOT circuit which follows two of the symbols.

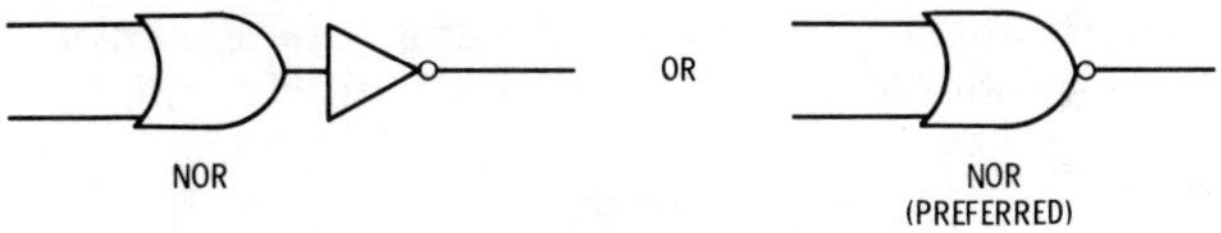

Fig. 2-4. Symbol for NOR gate.

Fig. 2-5 shows a transistor circuit capable of performing the NAND logic operation. In Fig. 2-5, Q1 and Q2 are npn transistors which will conduct if their base is positive with respect to their emitter. Notice that the Q1 collector provides the output for the

Fig. 2-5. NAND circuit.

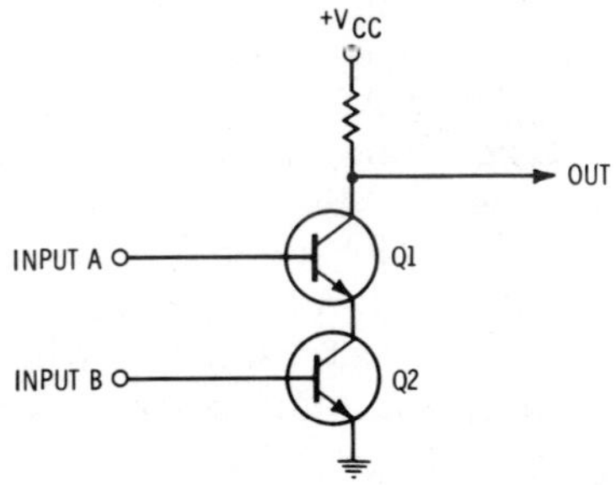

circuit. Current must flow through both transistors for an output signal to be generated, and when this occurs, the collector of Q1 is essentially shorted to ground. Therefore, when both Q1 and Q2 are conducting (or when a positive signal is present at the base of both Q1 and Q2), the output is a low voltage of perhaps 0.6 volts (binary 0). When one or both transistors are not conducting (or when one or both bases have no input signal present), the collector of Q1 is not shorted to ground and retains a potential of approximately +V (binary 1).

The operation of a NAND gate can be better understood by considering a practical example. Referring again to Fig. 2-5, assume the A input is a 1 state (high or positive voltage) and the B input is a 0 state (low or zero voltage). The positive voltage on input A will attempt to cause Q1 to conduct, but conduction will be prevented by the 0 state on input B. Therefore, neither transistor conducts and the output stays in the 1 state.

Thus far we have demonstrated one logic condition for a NAND gate: a 1 on one input and a 0 on the other gives a 1 on the output. Now assume both inputs are at a 1 state. A 1 at the base of both Q1 and Q2 will cause both transistors to conduct, thus shorting the collector of Q1 to ground and giving a 0 on the output. Therefore, a second logic condition for the NAND gate has been identified: a 1 on both inputs gives a 0 on the output. There are two other logic conditions for the basic NAND gate shown in Fig. 2-5, and the reader should identify and solve both of them.

NOR Gates

Fig. 2-6 shows a simple transistor circuit which performs the NOR function. As in the case of the NAND gate, two transistors are employed, and each requires a positive signal at its base in order for conduction to occur. While the collector-emitter junctions of the transistors in the NAND gate of Fig. 2-5 are in series, the same junctions in the NOR gate are in parallel. If either transistor conducts, that is, if either A or B input is positive, the output will be shorted to ground and have a low or 0 state.

Consider the case where a 1 is on input A and a 0 on input B. The 1 on input A causes Q1 to conduct, which shorts the output to ground, resulting in a low or binary 0 output. The 0 input at B has no effect since the output is already 0. Therefore, an initial logic condition for a NOR gate has been identified: a 1 on any input of a NOR gate will result in a 0 on the output.

Consider a second situation wherein a 0 is on both inputs A and B. In this case, neither transistor conducts and the output re-

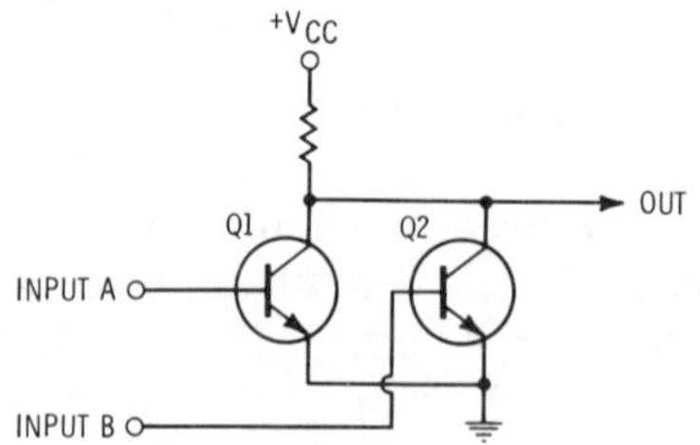

Fig. 2-6. NOR circuit.

tains a 1 state. Therefore, the second logic condition for a NOR gate has been demonstrated: a 0 on all inputs of a NOR gate results in a 1 on the output. There are two other logic conditions for the basic NOR gate shown in Fig. 2-6, and the reader should identify and solve both of them.

Reviewing NOT Circuits

Fig. 2-7 illustrates a very important concept of NAND and NOR circuits: a conventional NAND circuit can be represented by and is equivalent to a NOR circuit with zero-activating inputs (inverters). Similarly, a NOR circuit can be represented by and is equivalent to a NAND gate with zero-activating inputs.

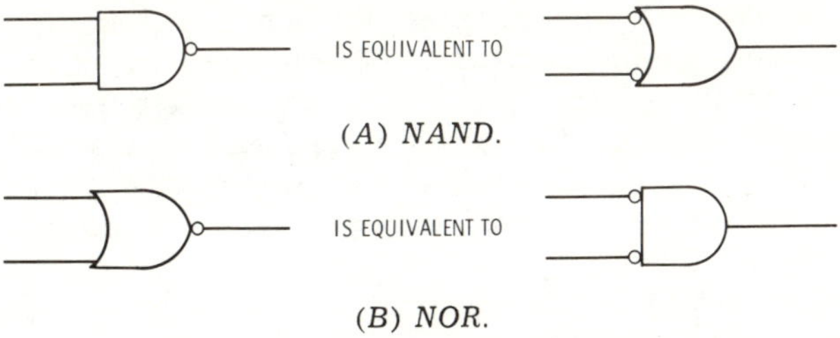

Fig. 2-7. Equivalent NAND and NOR circuits.

Binary Adder Circuit

Now that the basic logic circuits and functions have been explained, let's connect several together to form a practical system. Fig. 2-8 shows how several gates can be connected together to

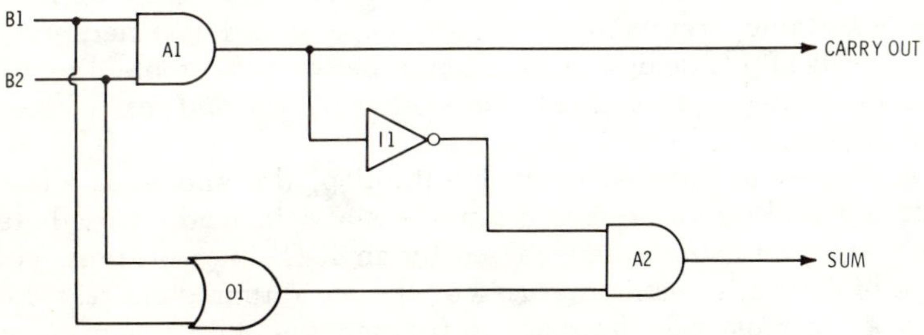

Fig. 2-8. A two-bit binary adder.

form a two-bit binary adder. To illustrate how this adder operates, assume that input bit B1 is a 0 and input bit B2 is a 1. A 0 and 1 into A1 will produce a 0 on the output, and this indicates there will not be a carry in the answer. The output of 01 will be a 1, and the inverter I1 will also have a 1 output. The two 1's into A2 will result in a 1, the correct sum of 1 and 0, on the output of A2. To verify operation of the adder, try other combinations and see if they result in correct answers.

Flip-Flops

Three classes of flip-flops are commonly used in computing circuits: bistable multivibrators, monostable multivibrators, and astable multivibrators. All flip-flops have two outputs, and these outputs are always complements of one another. For example, if one output is a 0, the other will be a 1 and vice versa.

Bistable Multivibrators—Bistable multivibrators have many forms, but all are characterized by their ability to maintain an output condition until this state is changed by a new input. This type of flip-flop is by far the most common in digital circuitry. It is used to store data in memories and shift registers, count, act as frequency dividers, remember status of logic circuits, etc. The most common bistable flip-flops are the J-K, the R-S, the T, and the D. It is beyond the scope of this book to discuss each flip-flop individually, but knowing that each changes its output state only when directed to do so by the input permits an understanding of any particular type. All that is required is to study the input logic table for each flip-flop in question. This information is provided by the manufacturer in the specification sheet of the device.

Monostable Multivibrators—The monostable flip-flop has only one stable state and always returns to this state a predetermined time after being activated. The time period is usually determined by an R-C time constant. Monostables are used primarily for synchronization and timing, and the number of them in a particular logic circuit are generally quite small in relation to the number of bistable circuits. In fact, many experienced designers judge the merits of a logic design by the number of monostable flip-flops it incorporates (i.e., the more used, the poorer and less efficient the design).

Astable Flip-Flops—The astable flip-flop, also known as a free-running multivibrator, has no stable state. Instead, it oscillates with a period usually determined by an R-C time constant. This type of circuit is commonly used as the basic timing generator or "clock" in most calculators. The frequency stability of most astable circuits is limited to about ± 20% in most production designs, and these relatively large errors prevent its use in precision timing circuits.

Typical flip-flop applications include counting and frequency division; operations which can be performed by a typical type-"T" flip-flop. The type-T flip-flop shown in Fig. 2-9 has the characteristic that whenever the input signal at T changes from a 1 to a 0

Fig. 2-9. Typical type-T flip-flop.

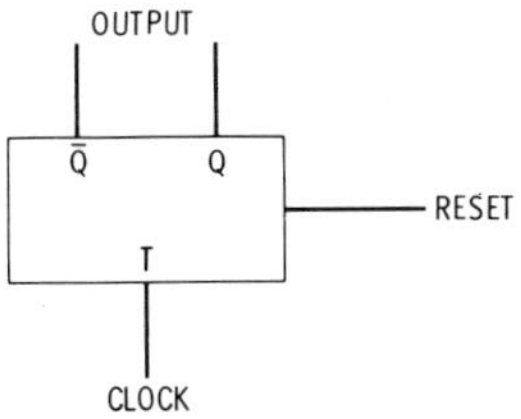

state, the output of the flip-flop will change. In the figure, the bar over output $\overline{Q}$ is read "not Q," meaning it is inverted from the Q output. The input labeled RESET will clear the flip-flop by setting the $\overline{Q}$ output to 1 and the Q output to 0.

To see how a circuit containing only three type-T flip-flops can be used for counting and frequency division, see Fig. 2-10. Fig. 2-11 is a timing diagram which shows the relationship of the flip-flop outputs (Q) to one another and to the input signal.

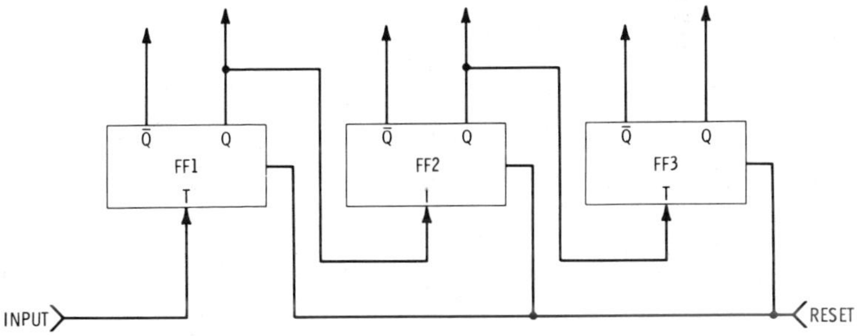

Fig. 2-10. Binary counter.

Before the flip-flops are activated, a reset pulse is applied to set all the flip-flops in the counter to 0. At t_0 the input signal changes from a 1 to a 0, and this causes FF1 to change from a 0 to a 1. Even though this output is fed to FF2, no change occurs on FF2, since a change can be initiated only by a 1 to 0 transition. After a time interval determined by the clock, the input signal changes from a 0 to a 1 again and there is no change in any flip-flop.

When the unit starts into the second cycle, i.e., changes from a 1 to 0, the input signal activates FF1, causing it to change from a 1 to a 0. This transition causes FF2 to change from a 0 to a 1 again with no effect on FF3. To see how the input signal pulses affect the various flip-flops and the resultant outputs, trace the input signal through the remainder of the cycles shown.

The timing diagram in Fig. 2-11 shows that the output frequency of FF1 is only one-half the input frequency. Similarly,

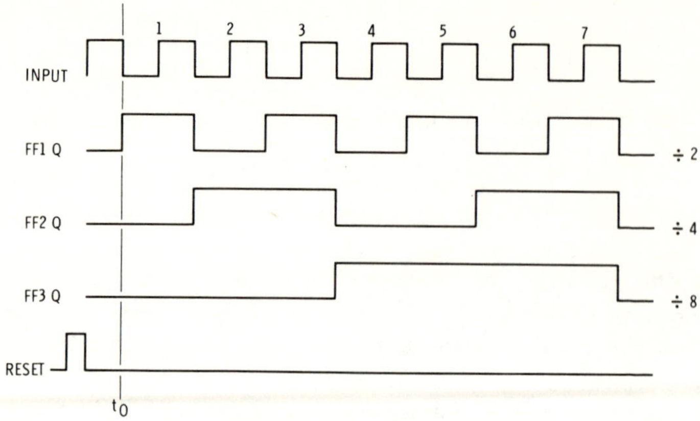

Fig. 2-11. Flip-flop output timing diagram.

the outputs of **FF2** and **FF3** are one-fourth and one-eighth of the input frequency, respectively. This clearly demonstrates the frequency-divider characteristic of the bistable flip-flop.

In addition to frequency division, the flip-flop chain shown in Fig. 2-10 is extremely useful as a counter. For example, consider the outputs of all three flip-flops after three input cycles:

FF3	FF2	FF1
0	1	1

011 is the binary equivalent of the decimal 3, the number of input cycles which have occurred. This shows that the flip-flops have counted the number of incoming pulses and have recorded the number by placing the least significant digit in **FF1** and the most significant in **FF3**. The counting operation can be verified by checking the output states during the sixth cycle (see Fig. 2-11):

FF3	FF2	FF1	
1	1	0	$= 6_{10}$

This concludes the discussion of electronic arithmetic and logic.

CHAPTER 3

Memories

All digital calculators and computers require some form of memory or storage device. Since digital devices operate in discrete steps, it is necessary to store intermediate results while subsequent steps are taking place. Memory devices are also required to store operating instructions and input and output data.

Memory functions are so important that digital devices are frequently defined according to their storage capacity. For example, the major organizational difference between a calculator and a computer is the superior size and flexibility of the memory of the computer.

Memories perform two major functions: storage of data and storage of instructions. Both functions are achieved by assigning the actual, or an encoded, numerical value to either the data or the instruction. Many different devices and techniques have been developed for this purpose, and one of the oldest and still most common is the punched paper card or tape. The common IBM card, for example, is simply a paper memory which conveys either numerical data or instructions to a data-processing device when the IBM card is processed through an appropriate card-reading device.

An early paper memory device is the paper roller used in player pianos. The data (instructions) to the piano are stored in the form of holes punched in the paper roll. Compressed air is incorporated as a readout mechanism. By passing air through the punched holes in the roll to actuate the appropriate keys, the piano automatically plays the tune previously programmed onto the roller. Automatic looms using this same principle were developed in the last century, and the technique is used in a great variety of control devices for automated production.

There are several disadvantages to mechanical forms of storage. The fastest card readers, for example, are extremely slow when compared to a high-speed semiconductor memory which can provide instruction or data within billionths of a second after being interrogated. Also, the card lacks an important feature known as *random access.* A random-access memory makes it possible to retrieve at will just one instruction or piece of data from any location in the memory. This feature is very important because it allows a computing device to modify its instructions as it makes decisions.

An IBM card only stores information for recall. A powerful memory system can be modified by the human programmer, central processor, or external data as needed. Size is important, and a modern semiconductor memory can store as much information on a silicon wafer $\frac{1}{10}$ inch square as a dozen IBM cards can. But it should be noted that present semiconductor memory systems actually store much less information in a given volume than it is possible to store in the same volume of paper due to the requirements of protective packages, control electronics, power supplies, and circuit boards.

Several terms are used frequently when discussing memories. A memory *address* is the location where information is stored. For instance, the central processor might instruct the memory to give it the information stored at location 743. This instruction will cause the memory to go to the address number 743 and retrieve the information stored at that location. An address, then, is simply a label given to a location in memory. Memories of primary interest in this book are *binary,* i.e., they store numbers in a binary format. Each binary digit is called a bit, and normally each address in a memory contains many bits. This collection of bits is known as a memory *word* or simply a word. Typical word sizes in a minicomputer are 16 bits. Data words in calculators, however, may be as large as 76 bits. Instruction words normally do not exceed 16 bits.

SHIFT REGISTERS

Shift registers are used as data memories and occasionally for instruction storage. The storage elements of a shift register are several flip-flops. Data is moved through a shift register by transferring data from one flip-flop to the next in a sequential fashion.

Almost all calculators are designed around large-scale, integrated (LSI), metal-oxide-semiconductor (MOS) circuits. The very high component density of MOS/LSI semiconductor circuits permits the production of large numbers of serial-in/serial-out shift registers on a single silicon chip. Because of the relative ease with which this type of data storage device can be fabricated, MOS shift registers are the most commonly used data storage units in modern calculators.

An important advantage of shift register storage circuits is their ability to literally shift bits through the register one at a time. This characteristic is called *serial operation.* Serial additon of two bits is accomplished by directly adding the two bits, while serial addition of multibit numbers is accomplished by adding each number one bit at a time and storing the result in an accumulator.

A typical shift register might use a type-"D" flip-flop such as the one shown diagrammatically in Fig. 3-1. This flip-flop stores the signal fed into the data input line whenever a control signal from an external timing circuit is applied to the clock input line. Fig. 3-2 shows a shift register which uses a serial array of type-D flip-flops. The input data is transferred into FFI when the clock pulse occurs. This causes the data from FF1 to be transferred to FF2 and the data from FF2 to be transferred to FF3.

Fig. 3-1. Type-"D" flip-flop.

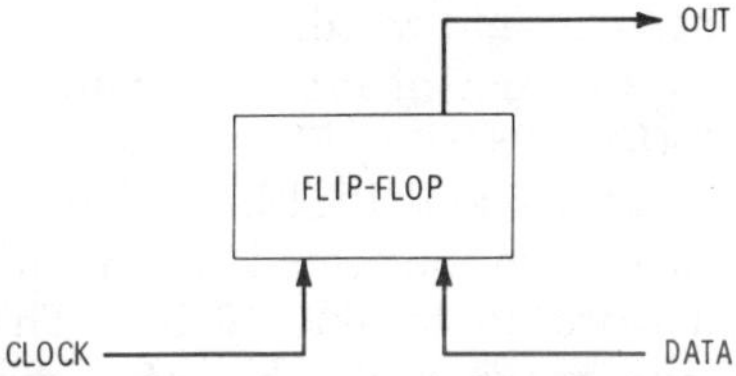

Shift-register types are identified by the way data is entered and extracted from the register. The example shown in Fig. 3-2 is a serial-in/serial-out register in which data is loaded and removed one bit at a time. Some shift registers are loaded and unloaded in parallel. This simply means direct access is available for each storage element. Typical shift-register variants include serial-in/serial-out or possibly parallel-in/serial-out registers.

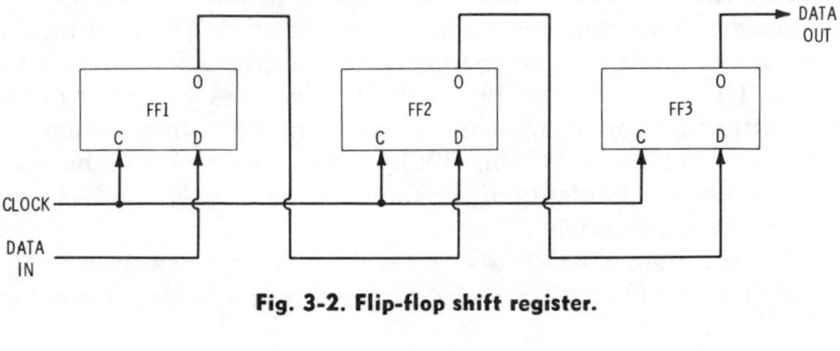

Fig. 3-2. Flip-flop shift register.

Serial-in/serial-out are the most commonly used shift registers in electronic calculators. Their use is normally limited to temporary data storage. Shift-register memories have the advantage of being relatively simple to build, and therefore their cost is low. They have the disadvantage, however, of not having instant random access, and a great deal of external control circuitry is required if they are to be used as data memories. Their popularity has been greatly reduced by improvements in MOS technology which make it possible to fabricate random-access semiconductor memories at prices that approach shift-register cost.

RANDOM-ACCESS MEMORY (RAM)

A random-access memory is a device which stores digital data in semiconductor flip-flops. Any flip-flop may be accessed directly. For that reason, it is possible to write into any location or read out of any location at random.

A complete conventional memory normally consists of a number of separate ICs each having one plane of memory locations and capable of reading or writing one bit of a word. Therefore, a 16-bit word would normally require 16 ICs each supplying one bit of the complete word.

The number of bits stored in each plane of memory is a power of 2 (64, 128, 256, 516, 1024, etc.), and the most common RAM sizes are 256 and 1024 bits. If 16 ICs each having 1024 bits of storage are interconnected, the result is a 1024-word memory with each word containing 16 bits. The memory chips have a built-in address register capable of addressing the appropriate memory location in each plane. There is also a control input which tells the memory whether to read or write. The RAMs are characteristically very fast; high-speed units can store or recall data in nanoseconds, while slower units require a microsecond or less. Their random access allows the central processor great freedom in control.

Unfortunately, RAMs have several disadvantages. They are typically more expensive than most other forms of memory, but this disadvantage will eventually be eliminated. Their storage is volatile, and the memory contents are destroyed if power is removed. This problem can be partially alleviated by using auxiliary battery power to keep the memory plane "alive" when the machine is not in operation. While the memory cannot be used in this mode, the contents of the memory can be retained at very low power consumption.

The RAM memories are also subject to the same environmental problems that affect all semiconductors (temperature, radiation, contamination, etc.). But this disadvantage is not a factor in most cases, since the environment must be controlled to protect external semiconductors even if the memory itself can tolerate a poor environment. It is almost certain that RAM memories will replace all other types of memories used in digital computers, but this replacement will not include bulk storage such as magnetic tape, discs, drums, and paper cards.

Fig. 3-3 shows a memory composed of seven 256-bit RAMs. An individual 256-bit RAM can be defined as a memory capable of

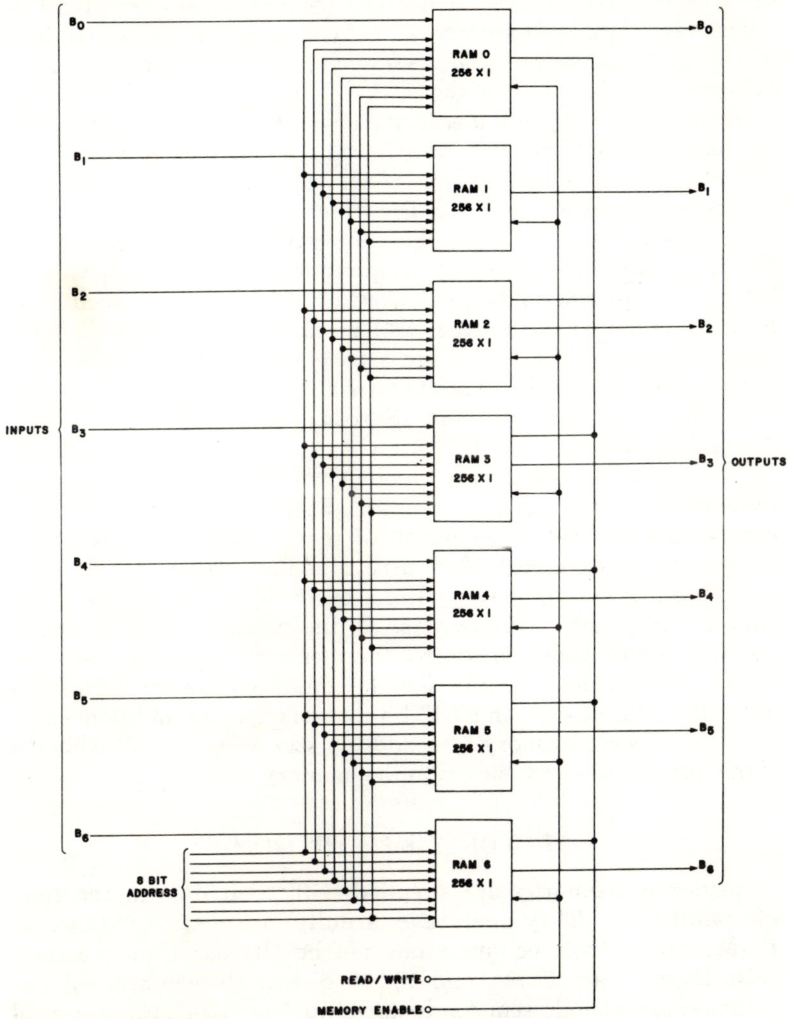

Fig. 3-3. Memory composed of seven 256-bit RAMs.

storing 256 words, each of which contains only one bit. Therefore, the memory array in Fig. 3-3 is capable of storing two hundred fifty-six 7-bit words.

Operation of the memory in Fig. 3-3 is straightforward. Each individual RAM receives an 8-bit address code. An 8-bit code is required since 256 corresponds to 2^8, and in order to address each location in the RAM, an 8-bit address is required. The address is fed into all RAMs via the inputs labeled B_0 through B_6.

Since a RAM is a read/write memory, a *read* or *write* command must be fed into the memory array by an enable line after the address is fed in. For example, a *read* command causes stored data to appear at the *output* lines. Similarly, a *write* command causes data entries to be stored in the RAM.

Normally the type of memory shown in Fig. 3-3 is used in a sequential mode, and a counter circuit automatically sequences the 8-bit address code through the RAM. This memory configuration is employed in the MITS Programmers to store program instructions for a calculator. The sequential technique permits a greatly expanded memory by simply adding additional RAMs to increase the number of bits per word. There is no theoretical limit to the number of RAMs that can be added to the fundamental circuit shown in Fig. 3-3. From a practical standpoint, however, the number of RAMs is limited by the drive capability of the *read/write* lines and the 8-bit address code required for the additional RAMs.

The number of words in the memory of Fig. 3-3 can be doubled by simply adding a second identical RAM array and a *memory enable* line to select from which of the two memories data will be entered or extracted. Two arrays containing 256 words each will give 512 words. Any multiple of 256 could be obtained by simply adding additional arrays. As the memory is expanded, a decoder can be added to control the memory which has been enabled. The memory enable signal would require an additional bit in the address code in a 512-bit memory and an additional two bits in a 1024-bit memory. The address size is equal to 2^n where n is the number of words stored in the memory.

READ-ONLY MEMORY (ROM)

Read-only memories are supplied with their data at the time of manufacture. They operate externally in the same manner as RAMs except their contents may not be altered. They are typically larger than RAMs, and 12,000 bits of storage are not uncommon for a single semiconductor chip. Fig. 3-4 shows a typical ROM chip.

Read-only memories are frequently used in calculators and computers to automatically generate certain commonly used formulas. For instance, to square a number with a calculator the operator presses a key labeled "x^2." The input decoder sees this key depression as a ROM address and causes the central process-

Fig. 3-4. Photomicrograph of ROM MOS chip.

ing unit (CPU) of the calculator to execute the instructions stored at this location. The instructions will probably tell the CPU to multiply the number in the display register times itself and then display the results. In practice, the instruction set would be more complex than this, but this narrative illustrates the general process. In actual practice, the multiply and divide operations are normally done by performing successive addition or subtraction according to an instruction set stored in a ROM.

ROMs have many advantages. They are cheap, fast, randomly accessible, nonvolatile, and consume little power. Their major disadvantage is that the contents may not be altered once they have been programmed.

PROGRAMMABLE ROMs (PROMs)

A programmable read-only memory (PROM) is a ROM which can be programmed by the user. The device as received usually contains the equivalent of a binary 0 at each of its storage locations. There are several types of PROMs, but the most common is the *fusible-link* type. This device incorporates a low-fusion material, such as nichrome or polycrystaline silicon, as one terminal on each of the diodes which comprise the memory array of the PROM. Higher than normal current passed through the array at selected points melts the fusible links and creates binary 1's as shown in Fig. 3-5. The current passed through the memory during normal operation is too small to affect the fusible links which have not been melted.

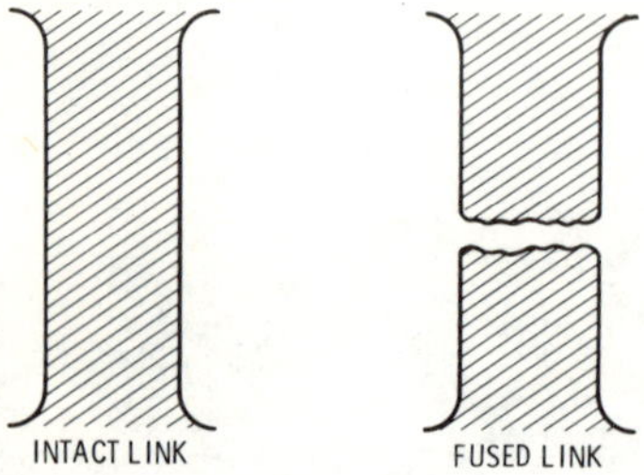

Fig. 3-5. Highly magnified section of fusible link PROM.

Conventional PROMs are programmed by the user in what is usually a single operation requiring perhaps a quarter of an hour. While the binary 1's stored in the PROM cannot be changed back to 0's, new 1's can be added by simply reprogramming the PROM. Because of their special construction, PROMs are relatively expensive and are therefore not ordinarily used in high-volume applications. They are, however, ideal for trying a design for, say, a new calculator memory without investing the large amount of time and money required for the custom mask necessary to produce a ROM. A PROM can be purchased, programmed, installed, and evaluated in less than a day's time. If it works properly and the resultant design is satisfactory for mass production, *then* a custom ROM can be designed and ordered.

MEMORY RELIABILITY

Typical semiconductor memory arrays contain thousands of interconnections, and it is the interconnections which form the key to reliability. By moving the interconnections from outside a chip to the chip itself, a development made possible by LSI technology, reliability is substantially improved.

Because of manufacturing trade-offs, there is an optimum overall chip area and number of storage elements for an individual memory chip. For example, yield, which is the proportion of good to bad memory chips obtained from a silicon wafer, falls as chip area increases. This is because there are fewer chips and each has more components. Similarly, as the density of components increases, yield also drops due to the increased complexity of each chip. To increase both yield and reliability, manufacturers have made careful studies of optimum chip size and component density.

An obvious reason for the importance of reliability is the great difficulty involved in pinpointing a defective memory. This is particularly true if only a few cells are bad. Frequently a defective memory will produce gross and obvious calculating errors when employed in an electronic calculator. But other times the error can be far more subtle and more difficult to detect.

Test jigs can check out a memory such as a ROM with little difficulty, but if the memory should become defective later problems will invariably occur. Defects are generally a result of improperly sealed packages which allow water or other contaminants to enter and affect the storage elements. A phenomenon unique to certain PROMs is "grow back," the reconnection of a fusible nichrome link by a self-restoration of the melted nichrome.

OTHER MEMORIES

Several classes of memory devices exist which may find use in electronic calculators. These include magnetic cores, and acoustical, holographic, and magnetic bubble memories. The first two of these memory types have already found application in some early desk calculators, but advances in semiconductor memories have greatly reduced their usefulness. Nevertheless, since some calculator applications may benefit from even the older memory techniques, it is appropriate to discuss them as well.

Magnetic Core Memories

Since the 1950's, magnetic core memories have been the mainstay of most large computer systems. A core memory consists of a matrix of tiny ceramic rings impregnated with ferrite oxide. Each ring or "core" is pierced by three wires, two of which control the magnetic state of the cores and one which senses or reads out the magnetic state. Fig. 3-6 shows a typical core-memory configuration. One-half of the electrical current re-

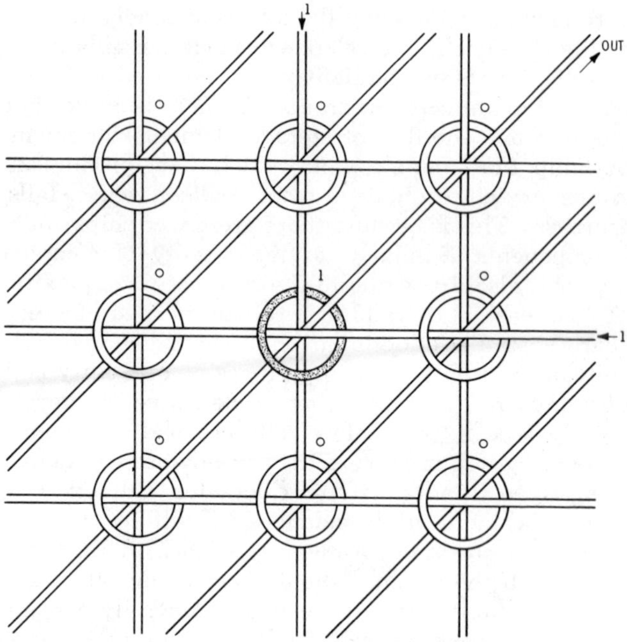

Fig. 3-6. Core storage array.

quired to magnetize a core is passed through each of the two control wires in order to impress a binary 1 on the core. The core stores the 1 until the magnetic charge is electronically removed and the core assumes a binary 0.

Core memories have been developed to a high degree of usefulness by the computer industry, but the fact that they are discrete devices makes them generally unsuitable for portable calculator applications. Each core must be individually and laboriously threaded into its matrix, and in a large memory, literally thousands of cores and connecting wires are required. A single array of cores is called a *plane* of memory, and a large computer may incorporate stacks upon stacks of planes. The best way to contrast core and semiconductor memories is to note that an LSI memory chip occupying the same surface area as a single core may contain hundreds of times the storage capability of the single-bit core.

Cores Versus Semiconductors

A major confrontation between the makers of core and semiconductor memories is shaping up. Cores represent a traditional and highly reliable approach to a nonvolatile memory. Semiconductors do not yet offer the nonvolatility of cores, but they are smaller, are easier to use, consume much less power, and are at least as reliable from a system standpoint. Since core-memory frames are used in virtually all major computer systems and since the calculator explosion has spurred on semiconductor-memory development to a highly competitive position, the conflict between the two is reminiscent of the battle between tubes and semiconductors.

At stake is a multimillion-dollar business, for memories, whether they be products of core, semiconductor, or other technologies, will find an ever-increasing role in consumer, industrial, military, and space electronics. Core makers are fully cognizant of the semiconductor threat and have responded by improving their own technology. Cores are now made smaller than ever, with 18-mil diameter units in common use. In past years, cores were laboriously strung by hand on frames containing hundreds or even thousands of individual cores. Now automated core-stringing equipment is being used by more and more manufacturers to speed up the assembly process and reduce costs.

New core-manufacturing processes are also being developed. Formerly most cores were made by a molding process, but some companies are now stamping cores from moving tapes of ferrite material. The result is a high degree of core-to-core uniformity, less production time, and lowered cost.

Even the traditional core material, a ferrite powder, is being modified to create new materials having more desirable properties. One result is TIN, an Ampex Corporation development. It is a temperature-insensitive ferrite material which can be operated at a much wider temperature extreme without external compensation than conventional ferrite materials. The result is higher density core planes. Ampex produces the largest core plane in the industry, a 500,000-bit frame.

Finally, sophisticated core-manufacturing techniques are being investigated in an attempt to produce a so-called "intelligent" or multistate core. In one approach, each core would consist of a nest of concentric rings bonded into a typical core configuration. By varying the number of rings in each core and adjusting the command and readout circuitry, number systems with bases other than two could be employed. For example, a decimal core would incorporate ten concentric rings. The associated control or write circuitry would have ten output levels, and the sense or read circuitry would be capable of resolving each level.

Promoters of intelligent core systems note that both auxiliary circuitry, such as binary-to-decimal and decimal-to-binary converters, could be reduced or eliminated if the new technique could be implemented. Furthermore, fewer cores would be required than in conventional binary-core memories.

Though it is likely that core memories can be made more sophisticated (as is being demonstrated by several major manufacturers), most computer manufacturers are closely studying semiconductor and other newer memory technologies. Many have already begun the switch from core to semiconductor and others are not far behind. In fact, almost all new designs employ semiconductor memories exclusively. Like the evolution from tubes to transistors, cores will not be eliminated all at once. In fact, some designers expect cores to be used for the next ten years despite advances in new memory technology, since a traditional and reliable approach to engineering is rarely abandoned overnight.

While some cores may be used in a few scientific calculators (even some yet to be designed), calculator design will most certainly depend upon semiconductor-memory technology. Computers will ultimately make the switch to semiconductors, but for now cores and other traditional memories like tapes and discs will maintain a strong competitive position.

Tape, Drum, and Disc Memories

The development of drum and disc memories paralleled the evolution of high-speed computers in the 1960's. Both memories consist of a rapidly rotating storage medium and one or more pick-off devices called sensors. Both are essentially highly sophisticated versions of the much slower magnetic-tape memory.

A modern drum memory has a storage capability of about 25,000 bits per square inch, while a disc memory can store up to 2,500,000 bits in the same area. While the capability for both devices is impressive, it is safe to say drums and discs are unsuitable for most calculator applications. The auxiliary equipment required to rotate the memory and the associated sensors requires more space than is available even in a large desk calculator.

This is not to say variations of drum and disc memories may not find limited application in certain calculator roles. New, sophisticated calculators may employ a variation of the disc memory called the *floppy disc*. Another possible avenue of research involves optical disc memories—glass plates photolithographed with tiny binary codes which supply information as diverse as complex instructions and which even have foreign-language translation capability. While an optical memory is limited to read-only capability, it can find use in areas requiring economy and ease of manufacture.

Tape memories are presently utilized in a number of programmable calculators for storing program instructions and data. Almost all such systems employ a miniature casette similar to those used in audio recording applications. Dozens or even hundreds of casettes can be made up and stored for use whenever needed. Fig. 3-7 shows a Wang 700 series advanced programming calculator equipped with a magnetic-tape-cassette memory. Notice the control keys for the tape cartridge in the upper right portion of the figure.

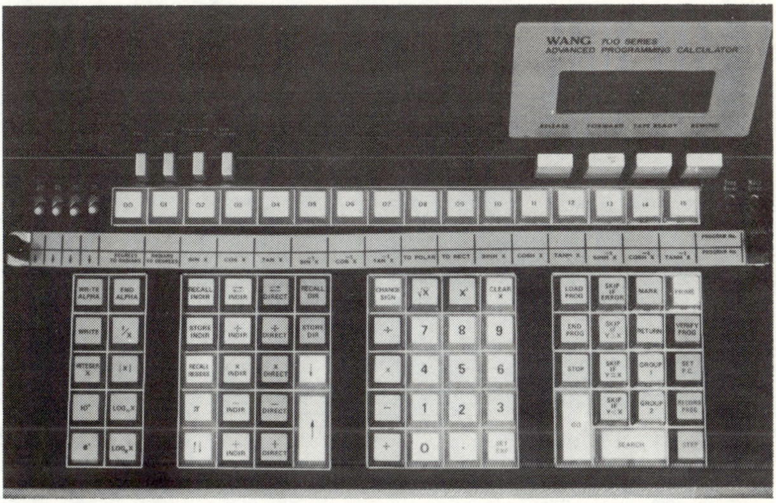

Fig. 3-7. Wang 700 series programming calculator showing magnetic tape-cassette receptacle.

Some calculators employ a variation of the magnetic-tape system. One incorporates a set of small plastic cards coated with ferrous oxide. The cards do not have the storage capacity of a typical casette, but they are particularly convenient for short programs. They are also easier to store. Fig. 3-8 shows the Hewlett-Packard 9810 a programmable calculator with magnetic-card-storage capability. A card is shown inserted in the read/write slot in the figure.

Amorphous Memories

Amorphous memories consist of thin films of a glasslike material capable of being switched from a low- to high-resistance state by an electrical pulse. Developed by Energy Conversion Devices, Inc., amorphous memories are also being studied by several other manufacturers.

The first commercial amorphous memory will be a 1024-bit read-mostly memory (RMM) produced by Energy Conversion

Devices. The device was originally developed by the firm for use in a solid-state crash recorder designed to monitor the impact of automobile accidents.

The 1024-bit memory is labeled a read-mostly device since it has a write speed of several milliseconds. Nevertheless data can be entered into the memory and erased at will, making the device significant for applications where slow speed can be tolerated.

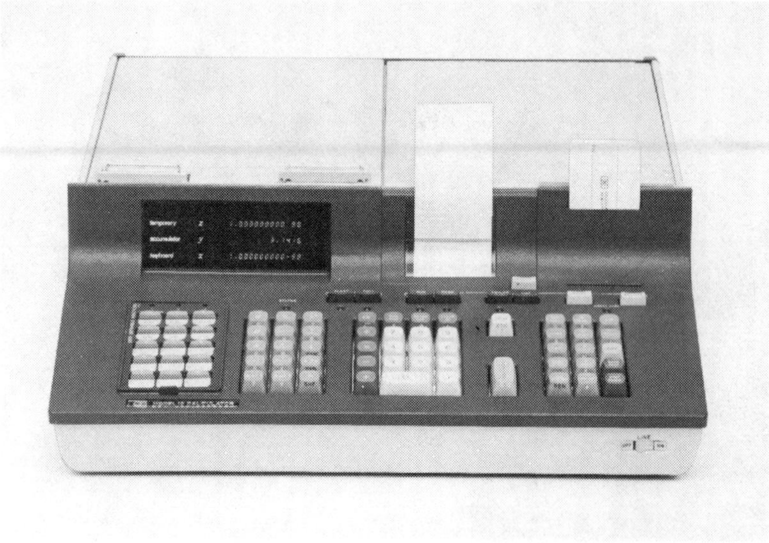

Courtesy Hewlett-Packard

Fig. 3-8. Hewlett-Packard 9810 programmable calculator showing magnetic card inserted into read/write slot.

Energy Conversion Devices is investigating ways to speed up the write time of its amorphous memory and has reduced it to 500 microseconds in experimental units. Since the memories are slated to sell for about the same price per bit as conventional PROMs, calculator manufacturers desiring to add a nonvolatile memory capability to their machines will be watching further developments closely.

Magnetic Bubble Memories

One of the newest memory techniques, the magnetic bubble memory, was developed at Bell Telephone Laboratories. This memory is based upon the formation of a cylindrical magnetic domain in a thin film of crystal such as gadolinium-gallium garnet. The domain is stable and can be moved throughout the crystal film, erased, and reformed by an external magnetic field. Fig. 3-9

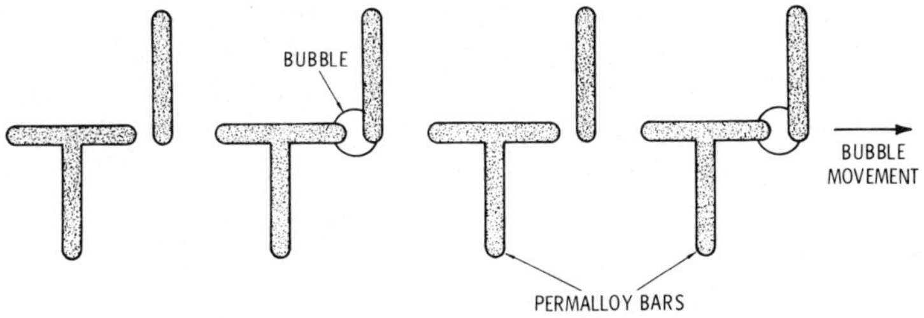

Fig. 3-9. A bubble memory in operation (highly magnified).

illustrates a bubble memory in operation. The figure is very similar to an actual photograph of a bubble memory since the bubbles can be made visible with optical techniques.

The major advantage of magnetic bubble memories is their small size. Researchers at IBM have built an experimental bubble memory with magnetic domains only 2 microns in diameter, and most workers believe the bubbles will ultimately be reduced to only $\frac{1}{10}$ of a micron in diameter. If this can be accomplished, a bubble memory with a storage capability of an incredible 10^9 bits per square inch could be fabricated.

Magnetic bubble memories are still in the early development stage with no foreseeable application to electronic calculators. However, it is interesting to contemplate the prospects of a calculator having the immense storage capability of a bubble memory. One problem remaining for bubble memories is the lack of a readout technique capable of sensing the presence of the tiny bubbles. One technique that is being investigated involves coating a special semiconductor readout array with the crystal in which bubbles can be generated. This kind of hybrid arrangement would be compatible with conventional semiconductor technology.

Holographic Memories

A new memory medium with read-only capability is the hologram. This memory technique exploits the ability of coherent light from a laser to impress large quantities of data into a photographic emulsion by means of interference phenomena. While holographic memories are limited only by the resolution capability of the photographic emulsion and can store a potential of 10^7 to 10^8 bits per square inch a laser is required to read out the data. Fortunately, low-cost semiconductor lasers can perform this operation but with less resolution (hence reduced data-storage capability) than larger gas lasers. Fig. 3-10 shows a diagram of an experimental holographic readout system developed by RCA.

Holographic memories offer potential advantages of reliability, simplicity, and ease of duplication. Already, practical versions have been demonstrated, and one pinhead-size film stores 20,000 bits. Still, the requirement of a readout laser restricts the application of this type of memory in calculator roles.

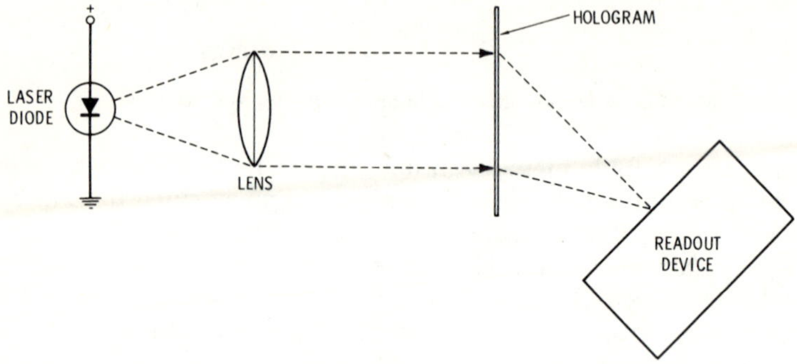

Fig. 3-10. Experimental holographic storage device.

Acoustical Memories (Delay Lines)

One of the first practical computer memories consisted of a mercury-filled tube with ultrasonic transducers at either end. By causing ultrasonic waves to be passed through the mercury medium data could be conveniently stored for later use. Fig. 3-11 shows a typical mercury delay-line memory.

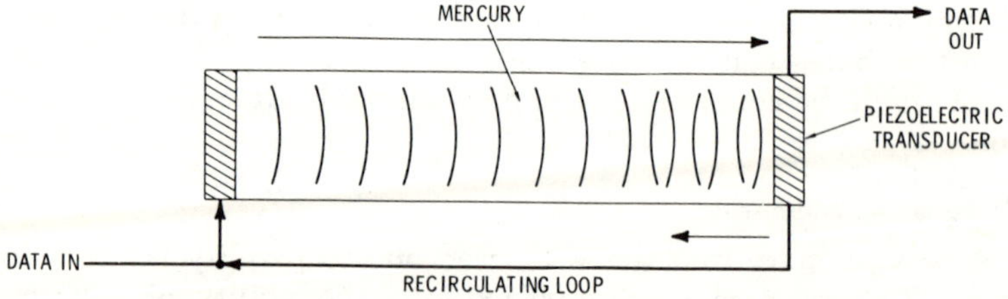

Fig. 3-11. Mercury acoustic delay-line storage device.

Modern acoustical memories are considerably more compact and sophisticated than this early method. Circulating-loop acoustical memories using glass or a variety of crystals and crystal films have been developed for use in desk calculators. Early Friden electronic calculators used a delay-line memory, and Sperry has perfected an acoustical memory with a recirculating frequency of 220 MHz and a storage capacity of 1280 bits per circulating loop.

The Future for Memories

Semiconductor memories retain a virtually insurmountable lead in present calculator technology, and there seems to be little chance for substitute systems in the simpler handheld and desk machines. Rapid developments in other memory techniques, however, may one day cause a swing to such sophisticated memories as the magnetic bubble. Meanwhile, the old standby magnetic memories of tapes, drums, and discs find widespread use in computers and some very limited use in a few advanced calculators.

CHAPTER 4

Calculator Organization

A calculator is an exceedingly complex device in terms of the amount of logic required to implement the functions available at the keyboard. Most of this complexity occurs in the MOS large-scale integrated circuitry.

In this chapter we will divide calculator organization into two major areas. The first area will be the MOS LSI circuitry, quite literally the brain of a calculator, and the second will be all circuitry and devices external to the MOS chip (s).

A modern calculator contains from 5000 to 30,000 or more transistor-type devices in one or more MOS LSI chips. Normally, the following basic organizational blocks are present in the LSI circuitry: the input decoder and storage register, the central processing unit (CPU), the data and instruction memories, and the digital display multiplex generators. External support circuits and components include the keyboard, power supplies (and/or battery charger), display buffers, seven-segment digital displays, and clock circuitry. Automatic power shut-off circuits are frequently included in handheld calculators. Occasionally keyboard debounce circuits are external to the MOS circuitry. Low-power detection circuits, which are almost always included in miniature battery-powered machines, are also external to the MOS circuitry.

The components external to the MOS LSI chip or chips are of most significance to the designer and repair technician, since these are the only portions of a calculator that lend themselves to troubleshooting and repair. A defect in the MOS LSI circuitry invariably requires replacement of an entire chip.

INPUT UNIT

The input unit receives signals from the calculator operator. In most machines this is accomplished with a keyboard. However, semiconductor switches, mechanical relays, and program input signals from an external programmer can also be used.

Two types of interconnection methods are used to connect the input unit with the keyboard in most calculators. These are the matrix type shown in Fig. 4-1 and the bus type shown in Fig. 4-2. The former is used in the MITS 908M and the latter in the MITS 1200. It is the keyboard circuits from these calculators which are shown in the two figures.

In a machine employing a matrix entry keyboard, the input unit sequentially scans each key to determine if a switch closure has occurred. As soon as the input unit detects a keyboard activity, it normally stops its sequential scan and waits to make sure the key switch contacts have stopped bouncing before accepting the key closure as a valid entry. The important advantage of this keyboard technique over that of the bus system is that fewer connections are required to interface a given number of keys with the input unit.

The bus system normally requires a separate input pin at the LSI chip for each key position. An alternative arrangement is to provide an external keyboard encoder to reduce the pin connections on the LSI package. The MITS 1200 series calculator, which is shown in Fig. 4-3, employs a bus entry with a diode encoding network as shown in Fig. 4-2.

Most of the newer LSI calculator chips incorporate automatic debounce circuitry in their input units. Debounce circuitry compensates for the tendency of most mechanical switches to "bounce" when closed. As shown in Fig. 4-4A, a switch closure does not necessarily result in an immediate contact. Instead, a series of momentary spikes occur for a few milliseconds until firm contact is made. Most logic circuits are fast enough to interpret the individual spikes as separate commands. Therefore, it is necessary to add a simple circuit which converts the initial switch bounce into a sustained closure signal. The result is also shown in Fig. 4-4B. If automatic debounce circuitry is not included in the LSI chip, the circuit designer must add a debounce capacitor or similar type of debounce circuit.

The input unit also provides a key storage device to compensate for rapid keyboard entries. If subsequent keys are depressed at a rate more rapid than that at which the CPU can process the incoming data and instructions, the keyboard unit stores these key strokes and releases them at a rate the CPU can handle. Very

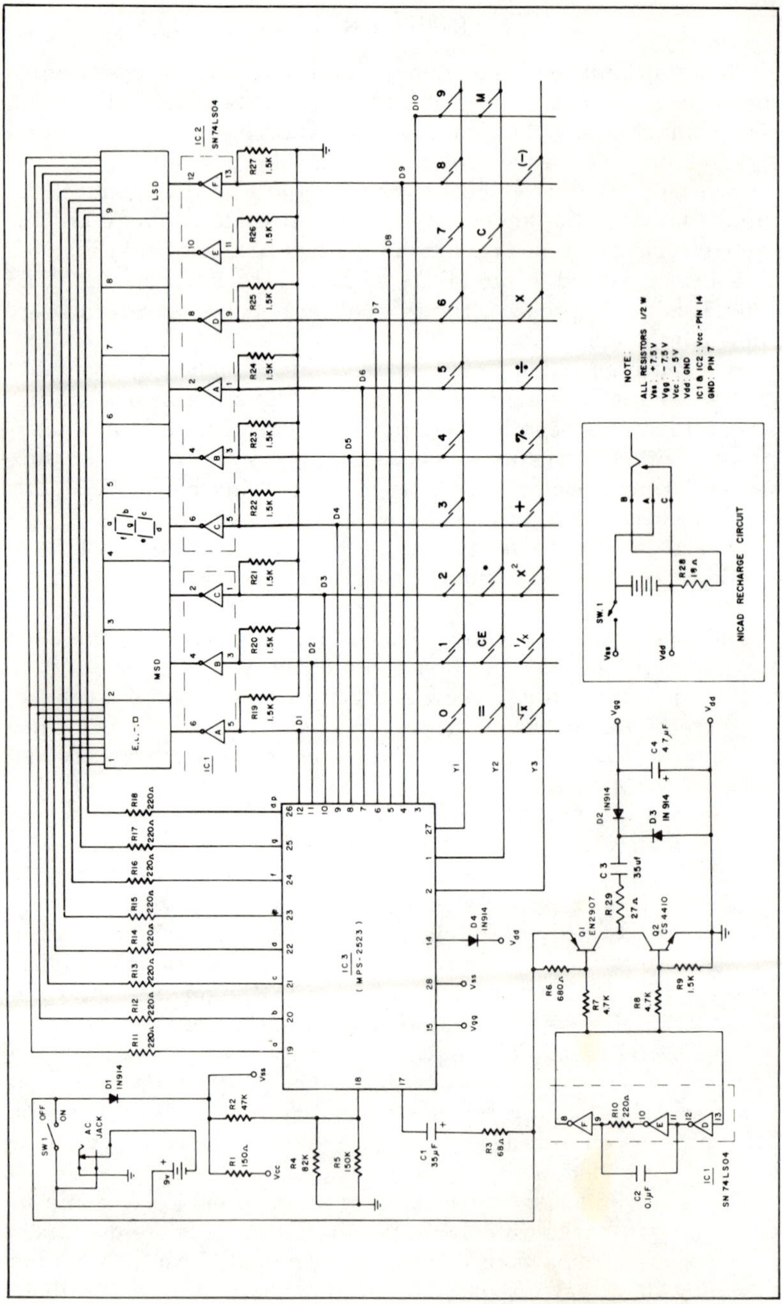

Fig. 4-1. Matrix keyboard circuit of MITS 908M calculator.

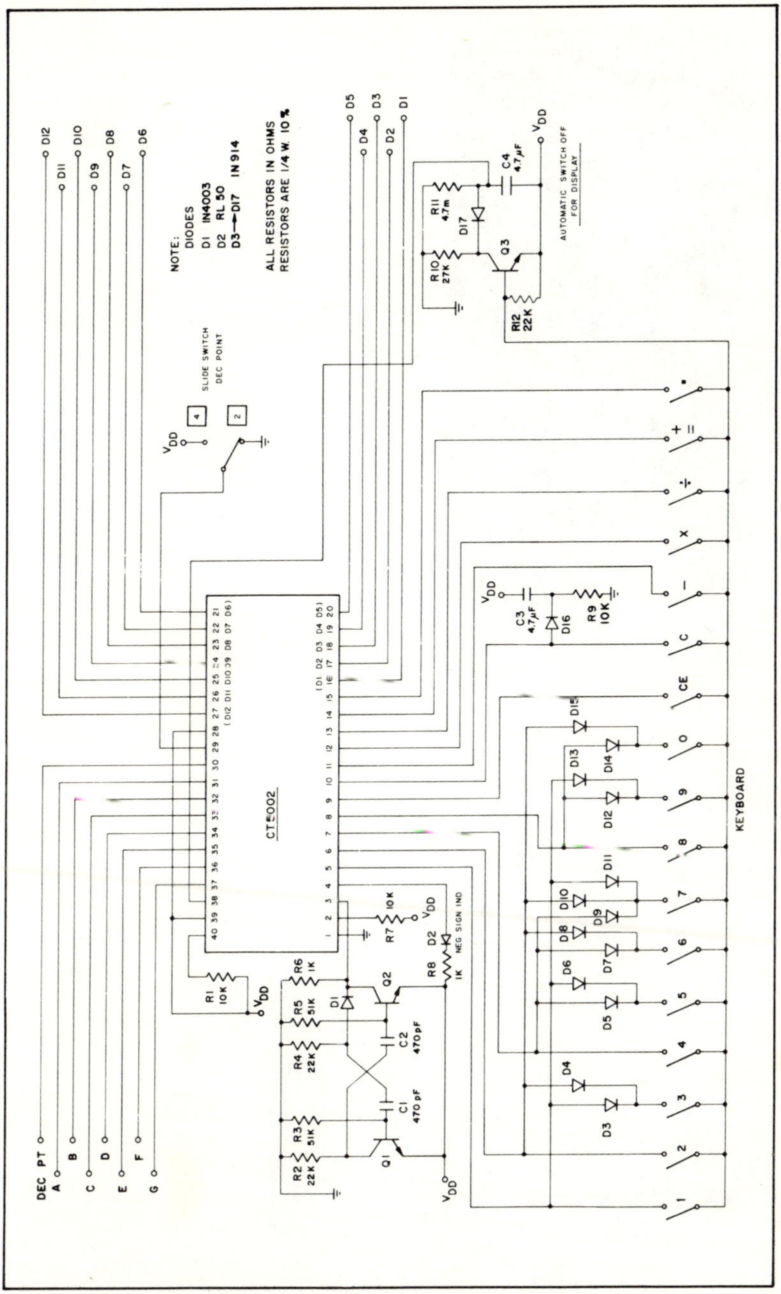

Fig. 4-2. Bus-type keyboard circuit of MITS 1200 calculator.

Fig. 4-3. MITS 1200 series miniature calculator.

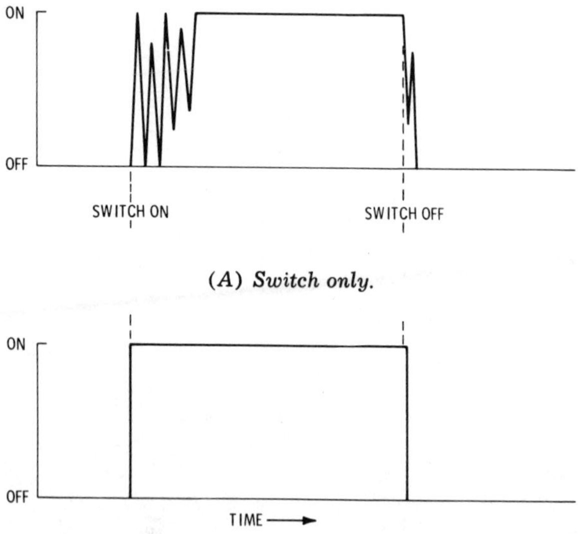

(A) Switch only.

(B) Switch plus debounce circuit.

Fig. 4-4. Typical switch contact bounce.

sophisticated calculators use a technique called "n key rollover," which permits any number of keys to be depressed sequentially and stored by the input unit until needed by the CPU. Most smaller calculators with simple designs have circuits that allow only one key to be stored at a time.

In addition to storing entries until they are required by the central processing unit, the input unit also solves the problems of simultaneous keyboard entries. The input unit automatically discerns the initial entry and ignores subsequent entries until that key is released.

The operational functions of the input unit are particularly important. When a key is depressed, the input unit determines if the key is a data or function entry. Data entries are the decimal point and the digits 0 through 9, and function entries are arithmetic instructions such as add, subtract, multiply, and divide. If the key is a data entry, the input unit routes the correct BCD code for that data entry to the appropriate register. If the key closure is a functional entry, one that requires a sequence of operations for the CPU, the input unit determines the correct starting address in the read-only memory for the required sequence of operations. The input unit also checks to determine if the CPU is busy. If the CPU is free, it activates the appropriate starting address in the ROM to initiate the stored microprogram instructions. The input unit does not provide data to the CPU until instructed to do so by the CPU.

CENTRAL PROCESSING UNIT (CPU)

As is already obvious by its frequent mention, the central processing unit (CPU) is the "brain" of a calculator. The CPU is where all arithmetic operations are performed, where data is transferred from register to register, and where timing and control signals for the remainder of the calculator are generated.

The major portion of the CPU is the arithmetic section. This section performs addition, subtraction, multiplication, and division. The arithmetic section of even the most sophisticated calculators is not capable of performing more than these four basic functions. In fact, the CPU of most calculators is only capable of addition. As discussed in Chapter 3, logic circuits can be made to perform three arithmetic functions by adding alone. Subtraction, for example, is performed by complementary addition. Multiplication is performed by successive additions, and division is performed by successive subtractions. Therefore, the entire arithmetic section of almost all modern calculators is simply a very powerful binary-coded adder.

Operation of the arithmetic section is straightforward. Typically, addition of two data words is performed by adding two BCD digits (two decimal digits in parallel) while adding the total word in serial. For example, the first digits of data words "A" and "B" are added together. If there is a carry, it is stored and the result is entered into the accumulator. Then the second digit of both data words "A" and "B" are added together, and the process continues until the complete data words are added together. The addition of each digit is accomplished in parallel, usually by a four-bit binary adder. It is important to understand that in most calculators the CPU is almost totally slaved to the read-only memory and performs only those operations which the ROM specifies.

MEMORY

Calculators normally contain two types of memory. One memory, usually a shift register, is used for data storage, and the second is usually a read-only memory. Programmable calculators employ still another type of memory, usually a random-access (RAM) or similar type of memory.

Basic four-function calculators store data words in registers, and a simple machine normally has three registers. The ROM is an unalterable permanent memory which stores the various instructions required by the CPU for the performance of any operation commanded by the keyboard.

Some of the ROM instructions are relatively broad. For example, an instruction might command "DISPLAY." This command causes the timing and control unit in the CPU to generate the appropriate display signals for a display. The generation of these signals may require a relatively complex sequence which is performed automatically upon receiving the ROM command. In general, however, each function in the CPU occurs a step at a time under the control of the ROM. Some typical instructions are "SHIFT DATA FROM REGISTER A TO B," "ADD CONTENTS OF REGISTER A TO THOSE OF B," etc.

Generally, the major operational difference between simple calculators (e.g., four-function units) and sophisticated calculators (e.g., scientific machines) is the instructions stored in the ROM. These instructions can be quite sophisticated. For example, they can contain algorithms, mathematical formulas which guide the CPU through the calculation of such functions as square root, logarithms, trigonometric functions, etc. Almost any mathematical formula imaginable can be approximated to a very high degree of accuracy by employing the basic four arithmetic functions. In a calculator, of course, this means almost any mathematical operation or function can be worked or solved by addition alone.

The first step in the design of sophisticated, special-purpose calculators is to design the algorithms required for the four basic arithmetic operations. From these algorithms the next level of complexity (e.g., X^2, reciprocal, etc.) can be generated without the need for redundancy. When the algorithms for problems of intermediate complexity have been generated, it becomes very easy to generate more complex algorithms since the latter can borrow from the former. For example, if the algorithm for $\sqrt{x}$ already exists and a more complex algorithm calls for taking the square root of the display at a particular point, the ROM can simply be programmed to instruct the CPU to refer to the square root algorithm already contained in its memory. In this manner, redundant and wasteful secondary programming is eliminated and more efficient use can be made of available memory space.

The reader has probably already noted that as more and more algorithms become available in the ROM of a calculator, it becomes progressively easier to generate additional functions. In fact, when sufficient "basic" algorithms are stored in the ROM, it becomes relatively easy to double the total number of available functions by simply adding additional instructions to the ROM microprogram. It is interesting to note that when a certain level of sophistication has been achieved in the ROM, the total number of functions is limited by such mechanical factors as case size and number of key positions and not the power of the calculator itself.

OUTPUT UNIT

The output section of a calculator normally provides three major functions:

1. Storage of the number being displayed,
2. Provision of the multiplex drive signals for the external display circuitry, and
3. Automatic decoding of the BCD data into a seven-segment format.

A typical data word contains sixty to eighty binary bits. This information is presented to the display one digit at a time. The process begins when the output circuit provides the drive signals for the first digit. The signal consists of the seven-segment drive commands and the digit selection itself. After a predetermined time interval, the output circuit selects the second digit and the process is repeated until the entire display has been completed.

A complete display cycle is called a frame, and a typical frame time for a modern calculator is from two to ten milliseconds. Since the display is refreshed between 100 to 500 times each second, it appears to be on continuously to the human eye, and there is no digit flicker unless the display is rapidly moved or vibrated.

Since MOS circuitry operates at extremely low current levels, it is difficult to interface a chip to a display without the assistance of current buffers. The output stage provides these buffers. In fact, a significant percentage of the total available chip area is required just to provide the few transistors which serve as current buffers.

Older calculator chips do not provide internal current buffers and output decoding. Calculators using these chips must, therefore, include external decoders to convert the BCD data from the calculator circuitry into a decimal format. In most cases this is done with TTL logic. The MITS 816 and 1440 calculators, for example, employ a single 7447 BCD-to-seven segment decoder IC for this purpose.

REVIEWING THE LSI CIRCUITRY

Fig. 4-5 sums up this discussion of the LSI circuitry in a calculator by showing the general relationship of the various func-

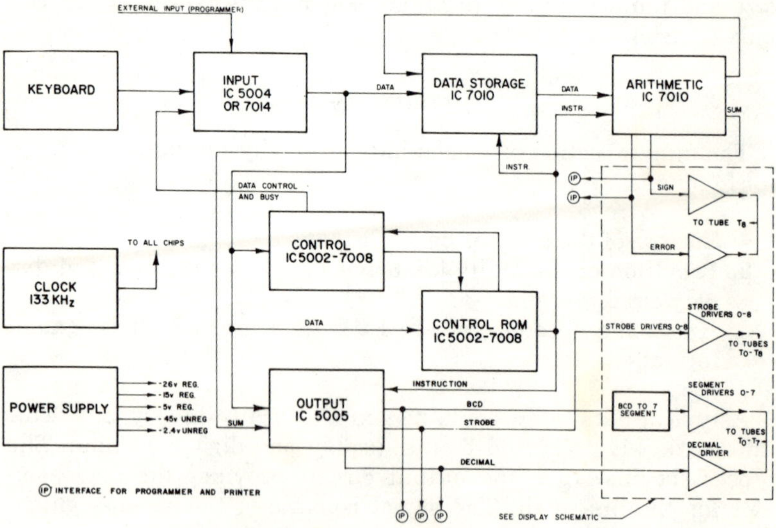

Fig. 4-5. Block diagram of MITS 816 calculator.

tions. Reviewing, the LSI circuitry contains at least the following basic functional blocks: input decoder and storage register, central processing unit, data and instruction memories, and digital display multiplex generators. This concludes the discussion of the LSI circuitry, and we can now proceed to those circuits and components which are external to the LSI chips.

KEYBOARDS

A keyboard is nothing more than an array of switches. Almost all calculators use various kinds of mechanical switches, but some use sophisticated optical and magnetic switches. Dozens of keyboard configurations are available from a variety of manufacturers, and we will consider several of the most important categories here.

Fortunately, the required specifications for a calculator keyboard are easily met. A typical calculator keyboard specification, for example, requires a closure (on) resistance of less than 100 ohms, an open (off) resistance of greater than 10,000 ohms, and a bounce time of five milliseconds or less. The resistance specifications are very easy to achieve. Typical keyboard switches have an on resistance of less than one ohm, while the off resistance is well over a megohm. In fact, the on and off resistance of most modern switches are a fraction of an ohm and many megohms, respectively, so almost any switch will meet the resistance requirements.

Bounce specifications can be more difficult to meet. Typical mechanical switches tested at MITS exhibit bounce times of about 100 and as much as 500 milliseconds. Therefore, the bounce time requirement usually becomes the most important specification when choosing a keyboard. Keyboards with excessive bounce can cause multiple entries from a single keyboard entry, erratic operation, and unpredictable operations. A function key with excessive bounce can cause such unusual operation of a calculator that an inexperienced technician will tend to suspect a faulty chip.

DESKTOP CALCULATOR KEYBOARDS

Two basic keyboard designs are employed in most desktop calculators. One employs conventional spring-loaded switches at each key position, and the other employs flexible metal sheets separated from a contact board by a perforated Mylar insulator. The former technique is advantaged by a high degree of reliability while the latter is characterized by low cost.

A typical keyboard employing spring-loaded switches is shown in Fig. 4-6. Frequent calculator users almost always prefer this kind of switch due to its "feel." The benefits of such physiological feedback are well known in many areas of endeavor requiring manual dexterity. Fig. 4-7 shows an internal view of a typical spring-loaded switch from a single key position on a keyboard. The number of individual parts in a switch of this kind and the quality of its construction explain the higher price.

Fig. 4-6. Miniature spring-type keyboard.

A typical keyboard using the flexible metal conductor approach is shown in Fig. 4-8. While these keyboards are quite economical, they are prone to excessive contact bounce and do not have the operating lifetime of quality spring-loaded switches.

MINIATURE CALCULATOR KEYBOARDS

The sophisticated, professional keyboards preferred for quality desktop calculators are much too large for miniature shirt-pocket machines. As a result, manufacturers have created a variety of novel keyboards which are thin, compact, lightweight, and reliable.

One simple mechanical keyboard is the snap-disc unit made by the Control Products Division of Texas Instruments. This keyboard uses a Klixon snap-action metal disc to provide the combined action of spring and contact bar. As shown in Fig. 4-9, when the convex-shaped Klixon disc is depressed, it makes contact with two conductive bars and completes the circuit. When the contact pressure is released, the disc snaps back to its normal convex shape and contact is broken.

Fig. 4-7. Internal view of single key position of miniature spring-type keyboard.

Texas Instruments is producing the Klixon keyboards in quantity for both its own use and outside sales. The board contains twenty individual switches, each having an actuating pressure of about six ounces. Contact bounce, a major problem in certain types of mechanical switches, is less than a millisecond.

Other features of the Klixon keyboard include a Mylar seal to prevent contamination, gold-plated contacts, and a total front-to-back thickness of less than a third of an inch.

The snap-disc principle provides the highly desirable combination of firmness and an audible indication of switching. Hewlett-Packard has adopted a similar principle for use in its HP-35 and HP-45 miniature scientific and business calculators. The Hewlett-

Fig. 4-8. Economical Mylar-type keyboard employed on early model of MITS 816 calculator.

Packard approach is shown in Fig. 4-10. A flexible metal strip is placed over a series of individual switching points. Slits in the strip permit raised points on either side of individual contact points to lift the strip at each switching point. When the raised points are depressed, contact occurs, and when pressure is released, the self-tension of the deformed strip springs the strip back to its raised position. The strips of switches required for a full keyboard are mounted on a printed-circuit board for convenient access to each switch position and for mechanical rigidity.

Sinclair Radionics Ltd. of Great Britain has developed a thin keyboard for its 2.5-ounce, low-power consumption midget pocket

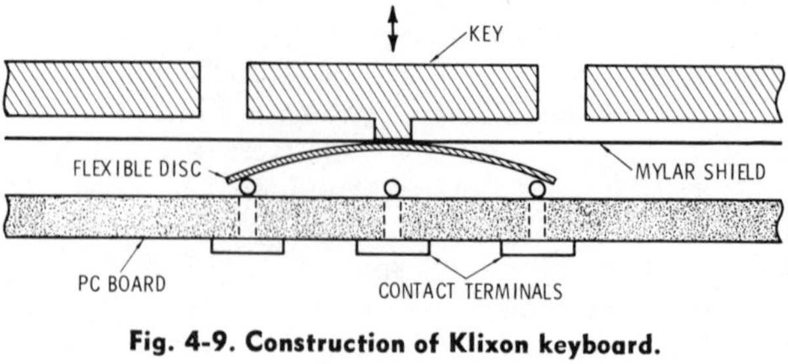

Fig. 4-9. Construction of Klixon keyboard.

calculator. The keyboard has no distinct keys as in the units described thus far. Instead, a flexible plastic coating is marked with appropriate symbols and digits. Switching action is achieved when pressure on each symbol actuates a gold-plated button contact behind the plastic layer.

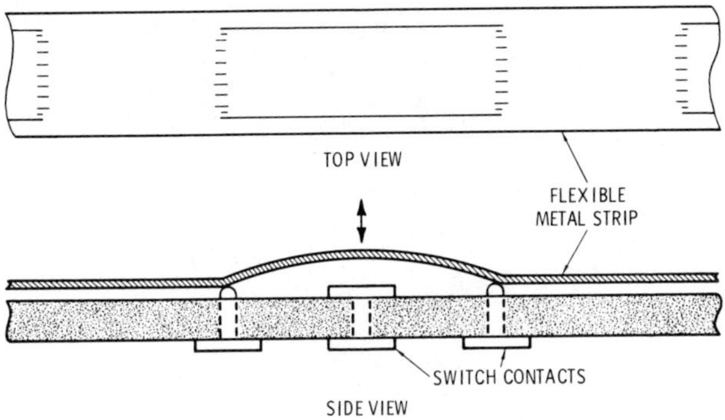

Fig. 4-10. Construction of Hewlett-Packard keyboard.

There are numerous other kinds of miniature calculator keyboards, but this brief discussion should suffice to show the general design trends. Perhaps the major change in calculator keyboards is the incorporation of dual functions for a single key. By pressing a special SHIFT key, the function of the remaining keys can be changed. The result is to almost double the keyboard capacity of even a miniature calculator. This keyboard change, of course, involves electronic additions to the calculator circuitry, but there are no modifications to the keyboard itself other than the addition of the SHIFT key and the secondary function markings.

Miniature calculators employing the shift-key technique are manufactured by Hewlett-Packard, MITS, and other firms. The MITS 941 Metric Converter calculator, for example, incorporates 41 distinct functions into only 20 keys, which include keys for the digits 0 through 9, decimal point, memory, clear, and clear entry. This calculator is shown in Fig. 1-14.

POWER SUPPLIES

The power supply for a typical calculator delivers as many as three separate voltages: a positive voltage for the MOS circuitry, a negative voltage for the LSI circuitry, and a voltage for the display circuitry. In some designs, particularly miniature models, all three of these voltages may be supplied by a single source. For example, the schematic of the MITS 1200 series calculator shown in Fig. 4-2 reveals that the negative voltage for the MOS LSI chip is actually ground and that the positive chip and display voltages are both supplied by a battery. This arrangement, however, is an exception, and usually three supplies are employed.

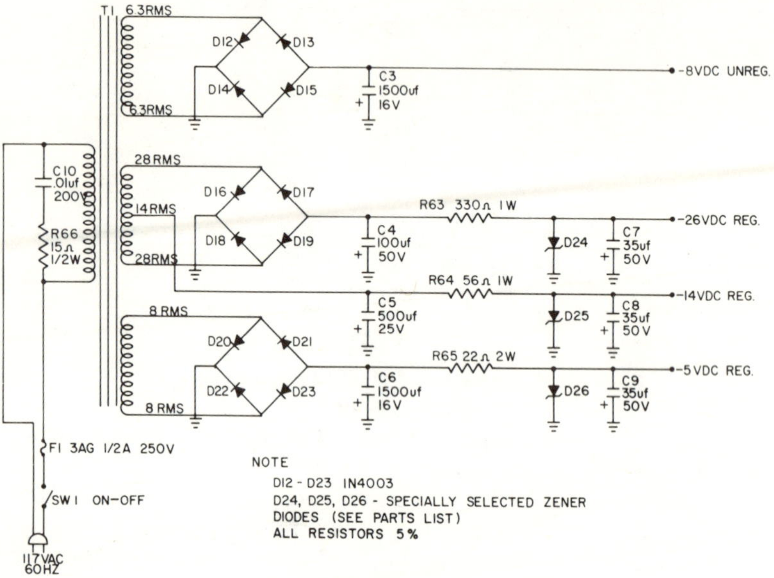

Fig. 4-11. Power supply circuit for MITS 1440 calculator.

Usually the power-supply voltage levels are not particularly critical to the calculator chip or chips, and a supply having a tolerance of only 5 or 10% is almost always more than adequate. The display circuitry is also relatively immune to power supply variations, though display brightness may be lowered somewhat should the voltage level drop sufficiently.

For these reasons the voltage regulators used in calculators are usually unsophisticated and, if present at all, consist only of zener diode regulators. Fig. 4-11 shows the power-supply circuit of the MITS 1440, a line-operated calculator. The capacitor section of the actual power supply is shown in Fig. 4-12, and the remainder of the circuit is shown in Fig. 4-13.

In handheld units, the positive voltage is supplied directly by the batteries and the negative voltage is supplied by a dc-dc power supply incorporating either a transformer-type inverter or a voltage doubler. Fig. 4-14 shows a voltage-doubler power supply.

Fig. 4-12. Power-supply capacitor board of MITS 1440 calculator.

Fig. 4-13. Main board of MITS 1440 calculator showing power-supply circuitry and six MOS LSI chips.

Calculators which employ battery power can use either a disposable or a rechargeable power source. On a weight basis, disposable batteries store approximately four times as much energy as nickel-cadmium rechargeable batteries. The latter battery, of course, has the advantage of being rechargeable and of requiring no periodic replacement. A typical pocket calculator, such as the MITS Model 908, operates about 38 hours from a set of good-quality alkaline cells but operates only 8 to 9 hours from a set of nickel-cadmium rechargeable cells.

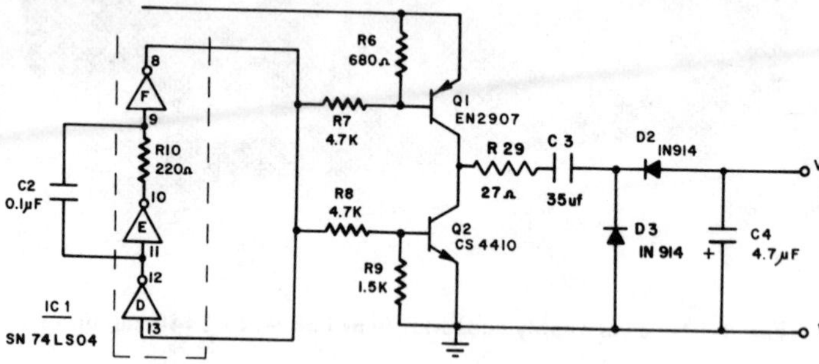

Fig. 4-14. A typical voltage-doubler power supply for a calculator.

Because of their high initial cost, many calculators use a smaller than normally required number of nickel-cadmium cells and voltage-multiplication circuitry to generate the required voltage levels. This means as few as three nickel-cadmium cells can be used in conjunction with several converter or multiplier stages to supply the required voltage levels.

Although these shortcuts are necessary to reduce cost, they also reduce the operating life of calculators employing rechargeable cells. Some calculators with as few as three rechargeable cells have an operating life of only two or three hours between charges. This is why the MITS 908 and some other machines use six rechargeable cells. Besides furnishing twice the energy, more cells mean a reduction in loss to the voltage converter or multiplier circuitry.

CLOCKS

Digital logic circuitry requires some form of driving signal. This signal steps the circuitry through its operational steps and causes counters to count, adders to add, dividers to divide, etc. The driving signal is provided by any of a variety of devices known as *clocks*.

First-generation electronic calculators required a two-phase clock, and some designs still require this type of clock. Second-generation calculators required a single-phase clock, and it is this configuration which is used in most modern calculators. Early single- and double-phase clocks were external to the MOS LSI circuitry. A typical external clock circuit is shown in Fig. 4-15. Now, almost all calculator chips contain integral clock circuitry in the LSI itself. This significantly reduces calculator complexity, cost, and size while eliminating a design problem for the calculator engineer.

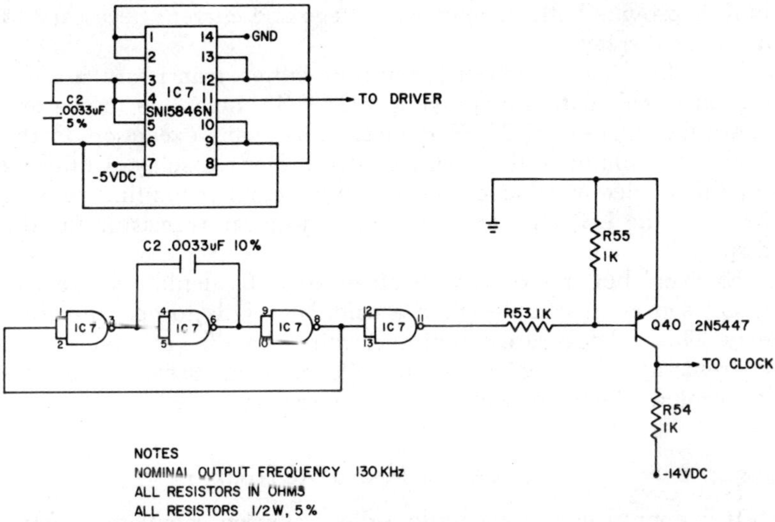

Fig. 4-15. External clock used with MITS 816 calculator.

Incorrect clock frequencies can produce erratic operation of the calculator, and in the case of external clocks, the repair technician should always check the clock signal and verify the following requirements:

1. Does the clock operate at a frequency within the specified frequency range for the MOS LSI chip or chips? The frequency range for most calculator chips varies from 25 to 500 kHz, so the only way to determine the correct operating frequency is to check the manufacturer's literature.
2. In the case of two-phase clocks, is the phase relationship between phase one and phase two correct?
3. Are the rise and fall times of the clock pulses within the limits specified by the chip manufacturer?

All three of these criteria can be readily evaluated with a general-purpose, dual-trace oscilloscope. Only in the case of external clock circuitry, however, can the repair technician remedy possible clock problems.

DISPLAYS AND DISPLAYS CIRCUITRY

Display devices and driving circuitry are discussed in detail in Chapters 5 and 6. From an organizational viewpoint, the calculater designer must ensure that correct buffering is provided between the MOS LSI circuitry and the display devices and that the buffers provide both the correct voltage and current necessary to drive the display.

With but few exceptions external buffer transistors are required in calculators employing MOS LSI chips, due to the low operating current of MOS devices. The main exception is the pocket calculator with a light emitting diode display. Buffering for this device is achieved with a single current-limiting resistor between the LSI chip and the segment-driver transistor for the display.

External buffer circuitry in all classes of calculators is a frequent source of trouble when a calculator fails to operate properly. This is because the buffer circuitry handles relatively high current, up to several hundred volts in some cases, which does not prolong the life of semiconductor circuitry.

CALCULATOR MANUFACTURING

It is appropriate to conclude a discussion on calculator organization with a brief description of how calculators are manufactured. The manufacturing process actually begins with the design of the MOS LSI chips that literally form the brain of the calculator. Due to the extremely high component density of these chips, their manufacture requires considerably more precision and care than that employed for less complex semiconductor devices. Therefore, relatively few manufacturers are engaged in their production.

When calculator firms design a machine, they can either specify a particular chip design or choose existing chips from a manufacturer's product listing. Since specifying a particular chip design can be quite costly and time consuming, almost all calculators use existing chip designs.

When a particular chip design has been selected, the actual design of the calculator can begin. Since the chip or chips contain all the necessary arithmetic, instruction, memory, and frequently display decoder circuitry, the design engineer can concentrate his efforts on the optimization of such areas as the power supplies and display drivers. Efficient power supply design is essential for portable machines in order to ensure reasonably long battery life, and good display driver design is required for reliable operation while maintaining a reasonably small component count.

When the design engineer has completed one and possibly more circuit designs, a *breadboard* machine is assembled. The design engineer works closely with the technicians who assemble the breadboard, for at this point, the need for one or more design modifications often becomes apparent. Sometimes design modifications are as simple as the addition of a single component, while other changes may involve an entire power-supply or display-driver circuit.

When the breadboard machine is operating properly and all known deficiencies have been corrected, the revised circuit design is given to one or more draftsmen who specialize in converting a circuit design into a printed-circuit layout. Often the same draftsman who produces the engineering drawings of the final circuit design is assigned to the printed-circuit layout, due to his existing familiarity with the project. Since calculator design often involves the use of double-sided circuit boards, a high degree of

Fig. 4-16. Draftsman preparing a calculator circuit-board layout.

competence must be exercised in the final layout in order to prevent costly and time-consuming redesigns. Fig. 4-16 shows a draftsman working on a layout for a calculator at MITS.

When the circuit-board layout is complete, a master photographic negative is made and actual circuit boards are made using a conventional light-sensitized resist. Completed boards are drilled and tinned to facilitate component installation and lead soldering.

Only a few circuit boards are made at this point, since another test of a working machine is necessary before committing the design to full-scale production. Using one of the boards, a technician assembles a complete machine, which is called a *brassboard.* If the breadboard tests and printed-circuit layout are perfect, the brassboard will operate perfectly and there will be no need for further changes or revisions. Due to the complexity of a calculator circuit, this is not always the case, and it may be necessary to revise the circuit design or, more likely, the printed-circuit layout.

Fig. 4-17 shows a MITS engineer performing evaluation tests on the MITS Programmer. Due to the complex nature of this

Fig. 4-17. Design engineer evaluating performance of a prototype calculator programmer.

device, several design revisions were necessary at both breadboard and brassboard stages; however, the programmer is now in full production.

At this point any necessary changes in the printed-circuit layout are accomplished and large-scale production of circuit boards is begun. Meanwhile, several other important procedures have been in process. Mechanical engineers specializing in the packaging of commercial electronic equipment have been involved in the design of a case for the calculator. Desk and pocket machines

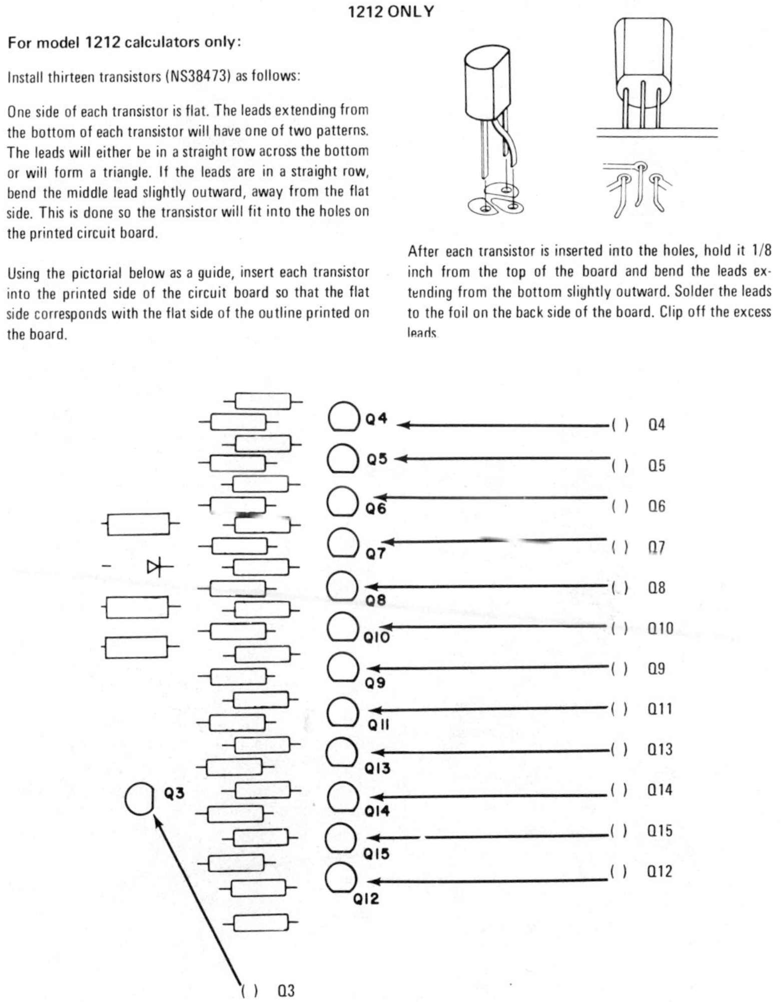
1212 ONLY

For model 1212 calculators only:

Install thirteen transistors (NS38473) as follows:

One side of each transistor is flat. The leads extending from the bottom of each transistor will have one of two patterns. The leads will either be in a straight row across the bottom or will form a triangle. If the leads are in a straight row, bend the middle lead slightly outward, away from the flat side. This is done so the transistor will fit into the holes on the printed circuit board.

Using the pictorial below as a guide, insert each transistor into the printed side of the circuit board so that the flat side corresponds with the flat side of the outline printed on the board.

After each transistor is inserted into the holes, hold it 1/8 inch from the top of the board and bend the leads extending from the bottom slightly outward. Solder the leads to the foil on the back side of the board. Clip off the excess leads.

Fig. 4-18. Page from calculator assembly manual (MITS 1200).

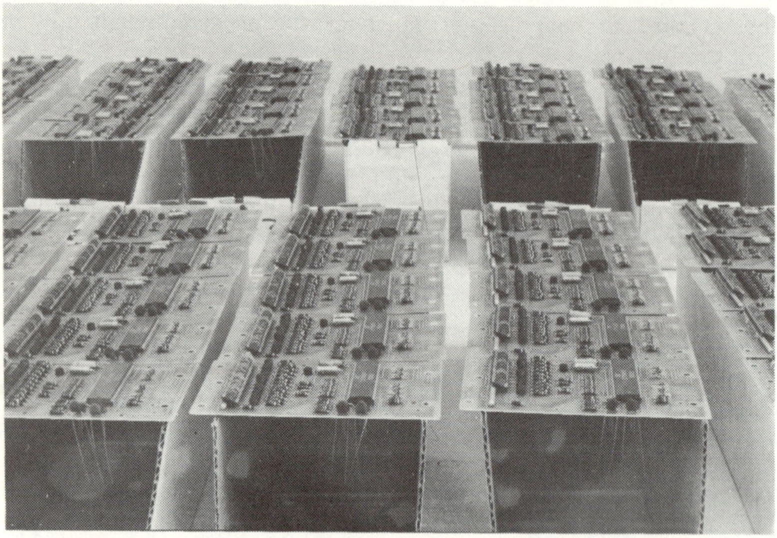

Fig. 4-19. Calculator circuit boards loaded with components and awaiting soldering.

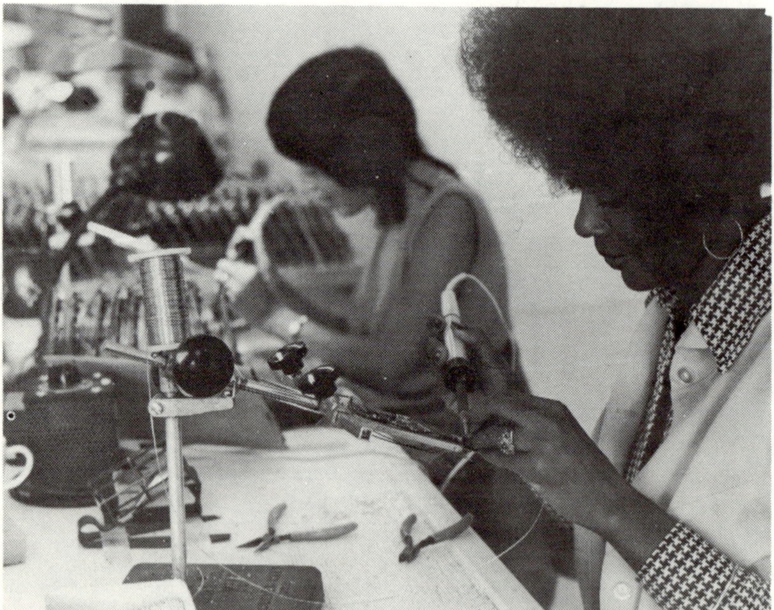

Fig. 4-20. Assemblers soldering components directly to circuit board.

present unique problems, so the package design is not necessarily the straightforward process it might appear at first. For example, pocket machines must be designed with very close tolerances to ensure minimum size consistent with mechanical strength. Pocket machines may also require different kinds of keyboards, displays, and plastics. Finally, pocket machines must incorporate provisions for internal batteries. Major changes in the circuit-board layout must be closely coordinated with the packaging engineers to avoid the possibility of too little, or possibly too much, space for the necessary components.

Another effort which is occurring at the same time as the circuit design is the procurement of components necessary for manufacturing the machine in production quantities. Due to the large number of companies in the calculator field and the general shortage of certain electronic components, parts procurement can become a major limiting factor in the transition from brassboard to production-model machine. There have been cases, for example, where a completed calculator design had to be abandoned due to problems in obtaining components critical to the operation of the machine.

Fig. 4-21. Technician loading loaded circuit boards into wave soldering machine.

Still another effort underway at this time is the preparation of operating manuals for the new machine. An even more involved procedure is the preparation of assembly manuals for calculators which are offered as kits. Fig. 4-18 shows just one page from a calculator kit instruction manual. The preparation of this page involves many hours of work and the step-by-step assembly of test machines to ensure that the instructions are totally accurate.

When the procurement of components for a new machine has been arranged and a target date for production set, advertising is usually begun. Several months of lead time are necessary here since that is the amount of time required for magazine advertisements to appear in print. Established manufacturers having customer mailing lists might also begin direct-mail advertising and promotion. Also at this point, one or more sample machines are sometimes sent to product reviewers at electronics magazines. If the reviewer is suitably impressed, he may write a column assessing the merits of the machine for inclusion in his magazine.

Finally, actual production of machines is initiated. First, as shown in Fig. 4-19, assemblers insert the various components into their respective holes in the circuit board. Mass-production ma-

Fig. 4-22. Rack of circuit boards just before arriving at wave of molten solder of wave solder machine.

chines are not soldered at this point. Prototypes and special-order machines, however, may be soldered as the components are installed, and this procedure is shown in Fig. 4-20.

Circuit boards loaded with components and awaiting soldering are loaded into racks on a special tray. When several trays have been loaded with boards, the boards are run through a wave soldering machine. This procedure, which is shown in Figs. 4-21 through 4-23, ensures uniform, reliable solder connections while minimizing assembly time substantially. As the tray of boards passes down a track, a carefully regulated wave of molten solder leaves a perfect solder connection at the juncture of every component lead and the circuit board. The solder boards are then removed from the rack and the excess flux is washed away.

Fig. 4-23. Circuit boards being automatically soldered by wave of molten solder. The smoke is from flux which is automatically applied to the lower side of the boards.

The completed circuit boards are inspected and then installed in their housing along with a keyboard, battery connection leads, and other appropriate components. The completed machines are then checked for proper operation and readied for shipping. Fig. 4-24 shows a batch of completed calculators.

Fig. 4-24. Completed calculators awaiting testing and shipping.

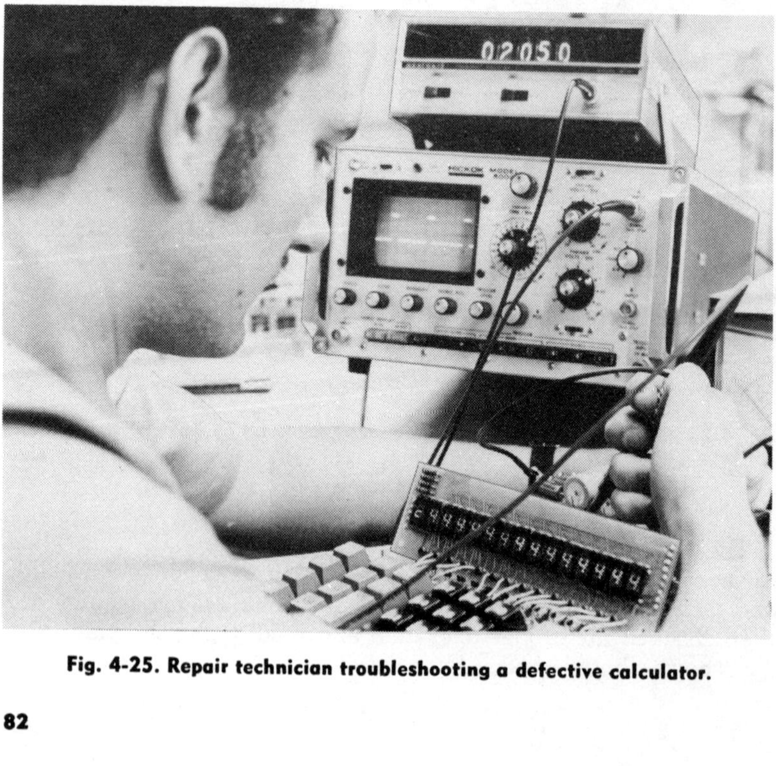

Fig. 4-25. Repair technician troubleshooting a defective calculator.

Fig. 4-26. Test rack "burning-in" repaired calculators.

Manufacturing is only part of a calculator firm's responsibility. Since no electronic equipment is 100% reliable and because the machines receive rough handling during shipment and sometimes during use by customers themselves, a calculator firm must maintain a complete service department. Fig. 4-25 shows a MITS repair technician troubleshooting a returned machine. Some repairs are quite minor and require only a few minutes of actual service time. Occasionally, a chip may be bad and require replacement. Repaired machines are normally operated for a designated time period before being returned to the customer to ensure that no other malfunctions exist. Fig. 4-26 shows a number of repaired machines undergoing an operational test. Many manufacturers operate several production-model machines 24 hours a day on a continuous-life test in order to find possible trouble spots and to study the effect of worst-case operating conditions.

In order to survive in a highly competitive market, the manufacturing process does not end here for successful firms. A continual watch on consumer demand and state-of-the-art improvements in calculator chips is maintained. When new developments occur which appear to have market potential, market surveys are made and, if the results are promising, the production cycle for new machines is begun. Frequently, a manufacturer will be introducing new calculators at the same time he is both marketing tested-and-tried earlier models and experimenting with completely different machines.

CHAPTER 5

Display Devices

Calculators are information-processing devices and, therefore, require a means for entering and extracting data. Almost all conventional calculators employ variations of the traditional mechanical switch in their entry device, the keyboard. But a far more diversified family of display devices is available for extracting processed information.

This chapter describes the operation of several popular display devices. The discussion of calculator output devices is continued in Chapter 7 with a description of several types of printers.

THE NIXIE TUBE

The Nixie tube, the first digital readout device to display actual numbers, was developed in the mid-1950's by the Burroughs Corporation in response to the rapid growth of the computer industry. Prior to the Nixie, the most popular readout consisted of a vertical row of neon lamps behind a translucent screen as shown in Fig. 5-1. The digits 0 through 9 were marked on the screen over each lamp. These early readouts could be mounted side-by-side to permit the display of multidigit numbers.

Vertical neon-lamp readouts were difficult to read since the indicated number zigzagged up and down the individual rows of lamps. The Nixie tube solved this problem by incorporating each of the ten digits stacked one behind the other in a single compact package, as shown in Fig. 5-2. Each digit is made from a thin-wire electrode with an appropriate outline, and all the electrodes are installed in a neon-filled glass envelope. By selectively energizing only a single element at a time with a suitable voltage, a bright orange-glow discharge in the shape of the desired digit is formed.

The Nixie tube was enthusiastically received by the electronics industry, and literally tens of millions have been put into service since its development. The evolution of semiconductor technology, however, has created a demand for displays with a lower operating voltage than the Nixie. Also, Nixie tubes are not easy to read as would be desirable since the stacking of digit electrodes causes numbers to appear to bounce back and forth within each tube. Since some digits are recessed more than others, the viewing angle is restricted. Another problem with Nixies is their tendency to "lock up" on one particular display. Finally, the orange color of

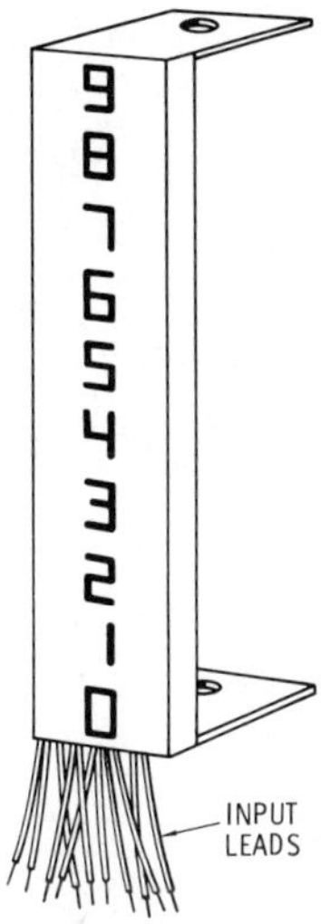

Fig. 5-1. A 0 through 9 vertical display.

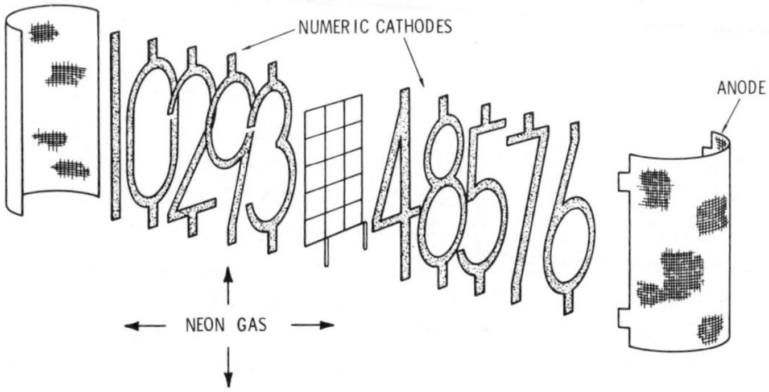

Fig. 5-2. Nixie tube construction.

the neon-glow discharge is not as pleasing as other colors. At the very least, it would be desirable to have a display with other color options.

GLOW-DISCHARGE DISPLAYS

The light emitting principle of the first successful numeric display, the Nixie tube, has been successfully applied to new seven-segment glow-discharge displays. Since the new displays utilize a seven-segment format, they are much thinner than the Nixie and its stack of individual elements.

One type of planar gas-discharge displays is the Panaplex II, a multielement unit made by the Burroughs Corporation. The device consists of two plates separated by a spacer. One plate, the anode, is transparent and contains one transparent electrode for each digit. The other plate, the cathode, contains a similar number of electrodes in seven-segment format. The device is fabricated so that the two sets of electrodes are directly across from one another when assembled as shown in Fig. 5-3.

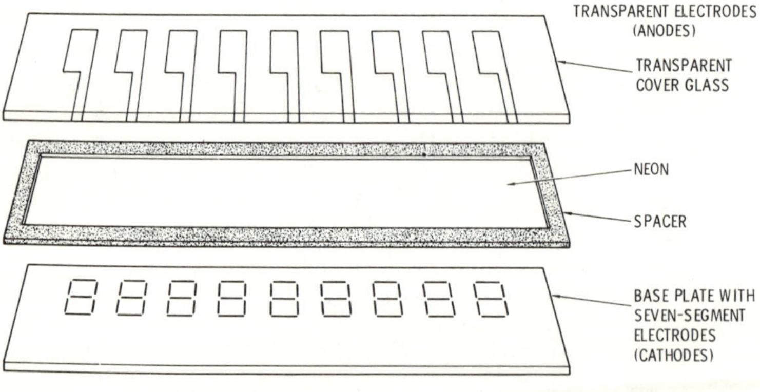

Fig. 5-3. Panaplex display construction.

Neon is introduced into the sealed space between the two plates of the Panaplex. In operation, the activation of appropriate anodes and cathode segments of each display in the array causes an orange-glow discharge to occur. The discharge is pleasing in appearance, and, since the neon emits a range of wavelengths, can be filtered to give a reddish color. Panaplex displays are available only in a multiplexed configuration at present.

Sperry also makes a seven-segment planar glow-discharge display. The Sperry displays are easy to read since the glow discharge extends completely across each segment, thus eliminating

Fig. 5-4. Sperry glow-discharge digital display.

the broken spaces which appear between segments of most other displays. The Sperry displays are available in a variety of sizes and in both individual and modular format. Fig. 5-4 shows a Sperry display in operation.

Glow-discharge displays have the advantage of high brilliance and ease of recognition. They are also quite economical; some units are available for as little as a dollar per digit in volume quantities. But like the Nixie, glow-discharge displays require a high voltage for proper operation. Up to 200 volts may be required. Fortunately, current consumption is relatively low so battery-powered calculators can use transistor dc-dc converters to obtain the necessary high voltage.

LIGHT EMITTING DIODES

All semiconductor junctions emit some visible or infrared radiation when forward biased. Gallium arsenide (GaAs) and its compounds are particularly efficient photon generators and have found widespread application as solid-state radiation sources, indicators, and displays.

Though more than a dozen semiconductors emit moderately efficient visible radiation when forward biased, gallium arsenide phosphide (GaAsP) is by far the best developed. The GaAsP light emitting diodes (LEDs) are particularly well developed and millions are produced annually.

Depending on the phosphorous concentration, GaAsP can be tailored to emit from the red to the yellow region of the visible spectrum. The most efficient operation occurs in the red at a wavelength of about 650 nm.

Gallium phosphide (GaP) is used for red and green LEDs. These diodes can be made to emit at very near the peak sensitivity region of the human eye (565 nm), but their hue more closely resembles a limelike greenish-yellow than a pure green.

Red-emitting GaP LEDs are more efficient than GaAsP diodes on a photon per electron basis, but the 690-nm wavelength of the material falls very low on the photopic luminosity curve. While GaAsP has a luminous efficiency of about 6%, red-emitting GaP has only half that value. Fig. 5-5 compares the wavelengths of several LEDs with the color sensitivity of the typical human eye.

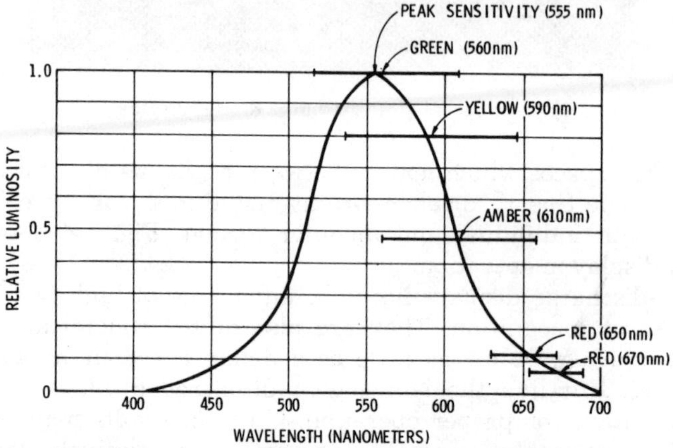

Fig. 5-5. Wavelength spread of common visible LEDs.

Both GaAsP and GaP LEDs can be multiplexed, but since GaP units have a relatively low saturation current, only GaAsP diodes are operated in a multiplexed mode in practical applications. This means red- and green-GaP displays must incorporate individual decoding and driving circuitry for each digit to achieve adequate brightness.

Fig. 5-6. LED display of Hewlett-Packard 9820 programmable calculator.

It is relatively easy to fabricate LEDs into numeric displays. Several construction techniques are used, but LED displays intended for calculator use are almost exclusively in seven-segment format. Some expensive programmable machines utilize a 4×7 or 5×7 dot matrix array format since they must also display symbols and alphabetic characters. Fig. 5-6 shows the LED display of a Hewlett-Packard 9820 programmable calculator which has a full alphanumeric capability. Special LED displays for the generation of characters such as the colon, polarity sign, error sign ("E"), and constant indicator ("C") are also available (see Fig. 5-7). The latter two symbols can also be displayed with a conventional seven-segment display.

(A) Colon. *(B) Plus/minus.*

Fig. 5-7. Special-purpose LED displays.

Price and visibility of an LED display are very much affected by the size and format of the individual emitting elements. For example, seven-segment displays incorporating only two individual diodes per segment use less semiconductor material than other displays and are therefore among the least expensive available. However, visibility is not as good as displays having more light emitting area per segment.

Currently the demand for LED displays is so great that prices have not yet fallen to the widely predicted $1 per digit. In recent years there have even been times when manufacturers of displays could not keep up with the demand for their products. With competition increasing, LED displays should be more plentiful and economical in coming years.

The LED displays emit less light than most other displays, and viewing can be hampered by poor contrast in the presence of bright ambient light. For this reason, all reflective surfaces inside the display package are usually blocked by black paint or special masks. Even the LED chip itself can reflect sufficient light to reduce viewing contrast, so frequently the display is cast in red epoxy, or a transparent red or polarizing screen is placed over the display. Even with these protective measures, LED displays are difficult to read in the presence of bright light.

LIQUID CRYSTAL

One of the most unique display devices incorporates a grease-like substance between two electrodes to produce digits and symbols. The substance is a *liquid crystal,* a large family of compounds having unusual electro-optical properties.

Early experimental liquid-crystal displays could not be operated in wide temperature extremes and had short operating lifetimes. Recently, however, operation over temperatures extending from slightly below freezing to nearly that of boiling water have been achieved. Also, new sealant techniques have been developed which keep the liquid-crystal material from seeping out of the display and shortening its life.

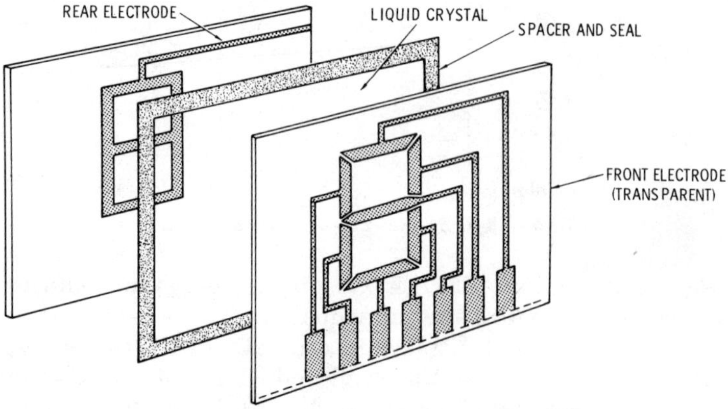

Fig. 5-8. Liquid-crystal display construction.

At present most liquid-crystal display technology is centered around two applications of *nematic* crystals. In the first, a thin layer of nematic crystal is spread over a flat electrode which serves as a ground. A sheet of glass containing a transparent seven-segment electrode pattern is then placed directly over the base electrode as shown in Fig. 5-8. A seal around the edge keeps the liquid crystal from leaking out of the display package. When a voltage is applied to the appropriate segments of the display, the normally ordered and clear nematic crystal becomes disordered and cloudy. If the back electrode is shiny, ambient light will cause the activated segments to appear white. This is called the reflective or passive mode of operation. An alternate mode incorporates a transparent rear electrode and a small lamp to illuminate the activated segments. This is called transmission or active operation. Fig. 5-9 compares reflection and transmission opera-

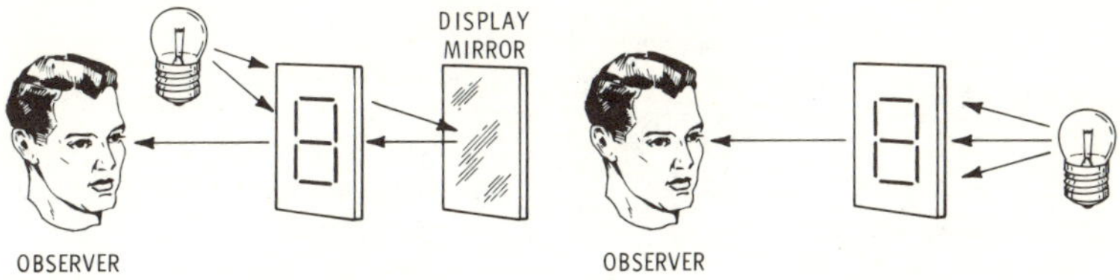

(*A*) *Reflection display.* (*B*) *Transmission display.*

Fig. 5-9. Liquid-crystal display modes.

tion, and Fig. 5-10 shows a calculator employing a reflection mode liquid-crystal display.

A basic nematic display operated in either the transmission or reflection mode normally requires at least 25 volts and consumes a few microwatts power. Best results are obtained with an ac voltage since dc tends to cause degradation of the crystal. The relatively high-voltage requirement has hampered the application of these types of displays in portable calculators.

Operation at much lower voltage can be obtained with a newer field-effect liquid crystal. The new display operates by changing its polarization in response to an applied voltage. By placing separate and crossed polarizers on either side of the display as shown in Fig. 5-11, the segments of a display can be made to appear.

Field-effect displays can be operated in both the reflection and transmission mode. They have a significantly lower voltage re-

Fig. 5-10. Calculator employing liquid-crystal display.

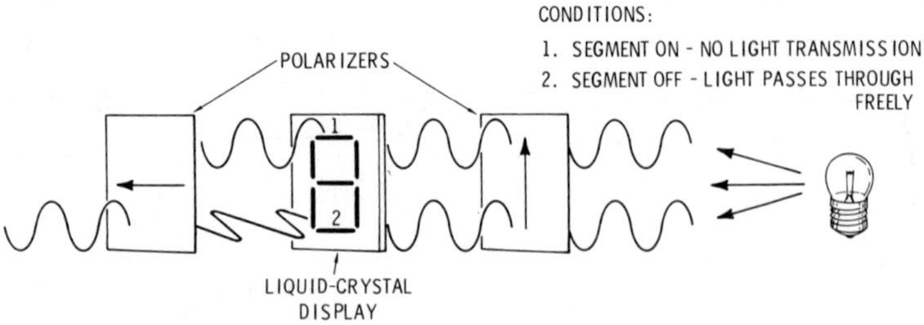

Fig. 5-11. Field-effect liquid-crystal display.

quirement, so operating power is less than the conventional liquid-crystal display. For these reasons, field-effect displays are expected to play a major role in portable calculators. A combination of MOS circuitry and a field-effect display will result in calculators having very long battery life.

A drawback of liquid-crystal displays is that they cannot be multiplexed without complicated driving circuitry. Also, their appearance is not as dynamic and attention-getting as displays which generate their own light such as LEDs and electrofluorescent devices. Another appearance criticism is their slow rise and fall time. The front and back electrodes separated by the liquid layer combine to form a parallel-plate capacitor which can store a charge. Therefore, the display does not respond as soon as an activating signal is removed. Instead it decays over a period of a few tenths of a second in a rather distracting manner. Fig. 5-12 illustrates this effect.

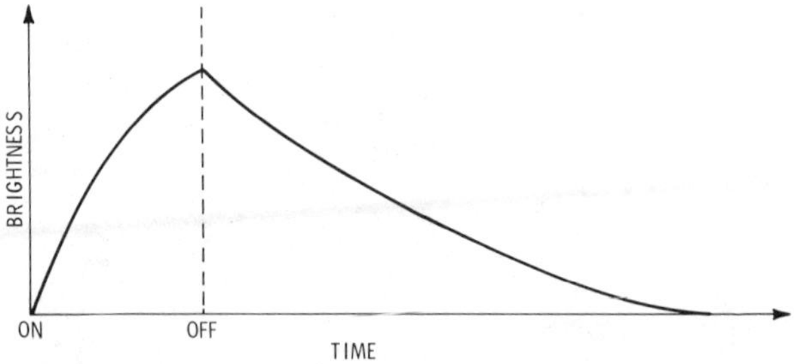

Fig. 5-12. Liquid-crystal rise and fall times.

Present liquid-crystal displays are limited by projected operating lifetimes of about 10,000 hours, but it is anticipated that new developments will increase this figure. Their disadvantages notwithstanding, liquid-crystal displays are being perfected to the point where they may soon become one of the most inexpensive display devices available. With less than 1¢ worth of active material required per display, liquid-crystal readouts are expected to sell for as little as 50¢, one-third the price of competing displays.

Though some calculator manufacturers have introduced machines with a liquid-crystal display, most are taking a wait-and-see attitude. The displays are plagued by reliability problems, and their appearance is not nearly as attractive as some other displays.

Nevertheless, the fact that commercial devices using liquid-crystal displays have already made an appearance despite their comparatively new technological and developmental status is highly encouraging and a portent for the future. Because of their very low power requirement, it is likely liquid-crystal displays will find widespread use in low-cost, vest-pocket calculators in coming years. Digital watches using a liquid-crystal display have already made an appearance, and an examination of the operating parameters of a unit made by Optel is a handy indicator of the remarkable capability of this display.

The Optel watch incorporates a four-digit display with colon, containing a high-purity nematic liquid crystal. To keep out contaminants and stop leakage, the display is hermetically sealed around its edges. Temperature compensation is provided by forming the edges of the display into a crescent shape to give room for expansion and contraction of the temperature-sensitive crystal.

The Optel display requires fifteen volts, a potential too high for most pocket calculators and all watches. A dc-dc converter circuit with 75% efficiency steps up the voltage from the 1.5-volt power cell by a factor of ten to achieve the required display voltage. A similar technique can easily be used in calculator applications.

The watch display consumes about 15 microwatts or approximately one-half of the total power required by the circuitry within the watch. The very low total battery drain, a result of CMOS circuitry, gives a battery life of approximately one year of continuous operation.

ELECTROFLUORESCENT DISPLAY

The electrofluorescent display is one of the most eye-pleasing readout devices available. Commercial units emit a soft bluish-green light which can be filtered to produce various shades of green and blue. Fig. 5-13 shows a typical electrofluorescent display tube.

Fig. 5-13. Typical electrofluorescent display tube.

Electrofluorescent displays are essentially special-purpose cathode-ray tubes. One or two heater wires suspended in front of a phosphor-coated seven-segment display emit electrons when connected to a current source. By energizing appropriate segments of the display, electrons are attracted to various combinations of the metal elements making up the display. The electrons pass through phosphor layers before striking the electrodes, and it is there where the light-generating process occurs. The phosphor atoms are stimulated to higher-than-normal energy levels by the electrons, and when they drop back to an unexcited state, photons are emitted.

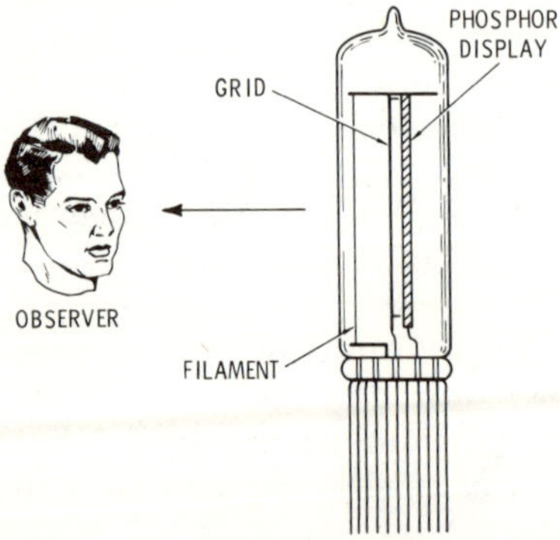

Fig. 5-14. Cross section of electrofluorescent display tube.

Since the electrons must penetrate the phosphor for fluorescence to occur, the filament wire (s) must be placed in front of the display as shown in Fig. 5-14. The small size of the wire causes no noticeable light blockage and is normally not visible.

Since they incorporate a filament electrode, electrofluorescent displays require two power-supply voltages of about 25 to 30 Vdc for the anodes and 0.7 to 2 volts for the filament. This is no problem for line-operated calculators, but the higher voltage does pose a drawback for portable devices. Electrofluorescent devices can be multiplexed, so they are desired for simpler circuits.

The major disadvantages of electrofluorescent displays are their inherent fragility, relatively large size, and high current consumption. However, these displays are so attractive that many desk calculators employ them. In volume quantities, electrofluorescent tubes sell for about the same as light emitting diode displays.

They are sold in arrays or as individual units which are then used to make up a display like the one in Fig. 5-15. While the latter technique requires more volume and expense, replacement of a defective tube is less costly than with a modular display since only the single bad digit need be replaced.

Fig. 5-15. Array of electrofluorescent display tubes.

OTHER DISPLAYS

The displays described thus far have been limited to those with the highest practical application to calculators. There are other displays which for a variety of reasons are not used in calculator displays at the present time. Since some of these displays may eventually be applied to calculators, it is appropriate to discuss them here.

One potentially useful display incorporates incandescent filaments in a seven-segment format. This type of display is inexpensive and can be operated at voltage and current levels compatible with integrated circuits. Normally the display emits a bright yellowish-white light but since an incandescent filament is a broadband source, colored filters can be used to produce a range of display hues. The major disadvantages of this type of display are its bulky size, fragility, and relatively poor appearance.

A particularly unique incandescent display manufactured by integrated-circuit techniques has recently been announced. Since this new display is housed in a compact, flat package and is inherently sturdy, it may find application in future calculator readouts.

A second class of displays which have not yet found practical application in calculators is the type that incorporates electrofluorescent powders and films. The best developed are electroluminescent powders made of zinc sulphide or other luminescent compounds. The powder is spread between two electrodes, one of which is transparent, and approximately 100 volts of alternating current are used to activate the phosphor. Both seven-segment and dot array displays can be made.

Light emitting film (LEF) displays incorporate a thin layer of luminescent material deposited on a transparent electrode. Voltage requirements are similar to the displays incorporating electroluminescent powders.

Both types of electroluminescent displays are very inexpensive (approximately 50¢ per digit in volume quantities), but their high-voltage requirement has limited practical application in calculators. There is a research effort to develop lower-voltage electroluminescent displays which will operate from direct current. If this work is successful, these displays might find application in calculator readouts.

CHAPTER 6

Display Operation

The output of a calculator, whether it be digital display or paper-tape printer, is one of the most important sections of the machine. Displays normally require at least as many connections as any other section of the calculator and in most cases consume far more power than all the remaining components of the calculator combined.

In order to simplify the operation of digital displays, calculator manufacturers use a scheme called multiplexing. There are several variations, but the basic concept is to time-share the operation of a decoder circuit among all the digits of the display in a sequential manner. Multiplexing, sometimes called time sharing, significantly simplifies the complex circuitry required to operate a digital display and, in turn, reduces both size and cost.

DISPLAY FORMAT

With the exception of some advanced programmable machines, almost all modern calculators incorporate seven-segment displays. As noted in Chapter 5, the segments can be generated with light emitting diodes, electrofluorescence, gaseous glow discharge, liquid crystals, and other light emitting or control methods.

The seven-segment font permits the display of the alphabetic characters A, B, C, D, E, F, H, J, L, P, S, and U in addition to the digits 0 through 9. Fig. 6-1 shows a typical seven-segment display font. Designation of the segments has been standardized in recent years; the uppermost horizontal segment is labelled A, and the remaining segments are labelled B through F clockwise from

A. The center segment is labelled G. In most calculators the decimal location is to the right of the seven-segment format, but in some calculators and digital instruments, the decimal is located to the left of the digit.

BINARY-CODED DECIMAL (BCD)

As noted in Chapter 2, binary-coded decimal (BCD) is the most usual manner in which numerical entries and solutions are processed by the circuitry of a calculator. Briefly reviewing, the BCD format used in most calculators is a four-place (bit) code used to represent the digits 0 through 9. The basic four-bit code can also be used to represent alphabetic characters by assigning numbers greater than 9 an alphabetic equivalent. For example, the number 10 can be used to represent the character A, 11 the character B, and so on to the number 15. Numbers beyond 15 require more than four bits.

BCD TO SEVEN-SEGMENT DECODING

It is relatively simple to connect a BCD circuit to an array of lamps to indicate the digits 0 through 9, but seven-segment displays are far more pleasant to view. Since the seven-segment display utilizes an array of bars to represent the ten digits, specialized decoding circuitry must be used when it is desired to convert a BCD signal into a digital output. The seven segments of the display must be actuated at the correct time and with only four bits of input data.

The decoding circuitry necessary to convert a BCD output signal into a seven-segment format is quite complex and typically requires some 72 logic gates. Fortunately, several transistor-transistor-logic (TTL) circuits have been devised which can perform the necessary decoding on a single silicon chip. One of the most popular decoders is the 7447. The advent of large-scale integration has further improved decoder technology, and now it is possible to fabricate all of the logic circuitry of a calculator, including the decoder, on a single LSI chip.

Decoder circuitry may or not have the capability to drive display devices directly. If it does, the circuitry is buffered and has the capability of withstanding the current and voltage required for the display. Nonbuffered decoder circuitry must incorporate external buffer transistors which switch the required current through the display. Each segment of a display requires a buffer transistor.

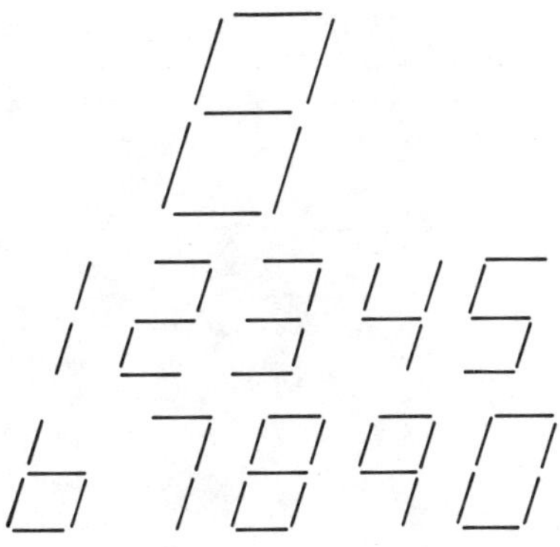

Fig. 6-1. Seven-segment display font.

MULTIPLEXING

The displays of almost all modern calculators are operated in a multiplexed mode. In the conventional or static operating mode, a separate decoder IC is required for each digit in a display. Since most calculators employ at least eight-digit readouts, the complexity, the cost, and the size of conventional operation can become excessive.

Multiplexing is a novel operating scheme wherein the individual digits in a readout time-share a single decoder circuit. The individual digits are activated one at a time in a sequential fashion until each display has displayed its respective digit. The cycle then repeats itself in a cycle faster than 60 times per second. Because of the persistence of human vision, the rapidly flickering display actually appears to be continuously illuminated and only a rapid movement of the readout reveals the sequential illumination of each display. An interesting experiment is to slow the clock of a calculator to actually see the multiplexing process.

Pocket calculators would be impractical without multiplexing due to the requirement of separate decoder ICs for each digit in the readout. For example, consider a typical display employing 12 digits. If each digit required a separate decoder, a total of 132 connections would be required between the calculator circuitry, decoders, and display devices. Fig. 6-2 illustrates the compact nature of a multiplexed display. The figure shows the entire LED display and multiplex circuitry of a Sharp pocket calculator.

In a multiplexed operating mode, all the A segments of each readout device are connected in parallel as are all the remaining segments (all the B segments, all the C segments, etc.). With this connection pattern, only one decoder IC is required to activate all the displays in a readout. Since the decoder has 4 BCD

Fig. 6-2. Sharp ELSI MINI miniature electronic calculator board and circuitry.

input connections and 7 output connections, only 11 connections are required to drive all the displays in the readout.

The multiplexing circuitry sequentially activates each digit one at a time. In a typical circuit, the multiplier begins its cycle by applying an activating signal to the first digit in the readout. While the seven-segment decoder IC may be transmitting a digit to all the display devices in the readout simultaneously, the multiplex control circuitry enables only one display at a time to be activated.

In a typical calculator display circuit, each digit in the readout is activated for about 300 microseconds. At the end of this interval, the digit enable line is disconnected by the control electronics and the next digit is activated for 300 microseconds. The process continues until all the digits in the readout have been activated and then repeats itself.

A conventionally driven 12-digit readout requires at least 132 connections. The same display operated in a multiplexed mode requires only 23 connections. Besides requiring only one decoder IC, a multiplexed readout can share any necessary buffer transistors among all the display devices. Many calculators, particularly the desk variety, require one or two buffer transistors per display segment. These segment-driver transistors, as they are usually known, would number either 84 or 168 in a 12-digit machine having conventional decoding circuitry. Since each transistor has three leads and since current-limiting resistors for each segment are frequently necessary, the total number of connections can be well over 500. This compares to 7 transistors and less than 50 connections for a multiplexed display.

Another significant advantage of multiplexing concerns the simplicity of manufacturing certain display devices. With conventional drive techniques, each connection to a seven-segment display must be brought out of the display package. The large number of leads required for a single-digit display, at least nine, precludes packaging several displays in a compact, easily installed package. Multiplexing, however, means all display segments are connected in parallel. Therefore, an array of readouts can be conveniently packaged in a single package which has only a limited number of leads.

While multiplexing may seem fairly complex, it should be obvious by now that it constitutes a major shortcut in display design and assembly. It is unlikely that calculator prices and sizes could have been reduced as much as they have in recent years without the help of multiplexed display circuits. In the remainder of this chapter, we will take a closer look at two major classes of displays—light emitting diodes and electrofluorescent display tubes—and describe their drive circuitry in detail.

LIGHT EMITTING DIODE DISPLAYS

Currently, light emitting diode (LED) displays are one of the most popular display devices for portable calculators. A typical circuit for driving an LED display in a calculator is shown in Fig. 6-3. The circuit is used in the MITS Model 1200 series calculators.

The lower portion of the circuit diagram in Fig. 6-3 shows a series of input lines designated G, F, E, D, C, B, A, DEC PT, and V_{SS}. The alphabetic characters correspond to each of the seven segments in the display, *DEC PT* is the decimal point, and V_{SS} is a power supply line. Resistors R45 through R53 serve to limit current through the LED display, a role which will be described in more detail later. The MITS Model 1200 is a late-model calculator which has a single MOS LSI calculator chip with self-contained BCD to seven-segment decoder circuitry. The decoder circuitry has sufficient drive to operate the LED segments directly.

A simplified version of a single segment of an LED display and its drive circuitry is shown in Fig. 6-4. The circuit consists of a drive transistor, a current-limiting resistor, and a single light emitting diode junction. The circuit is connected to an input voltage of approximately 7.5 volts, the resistor has a value of 220 ohms, and the transistor is an npn driver.

The 220-ohm resistor in Fig. 6-4 limits the current to the LED to a normal value. The value of the series resistor is selected by determining the multiplex duty and the required LED brightness. To increase battery life, power is conserved by operating the LED at much lower than the maximum allowable current level.

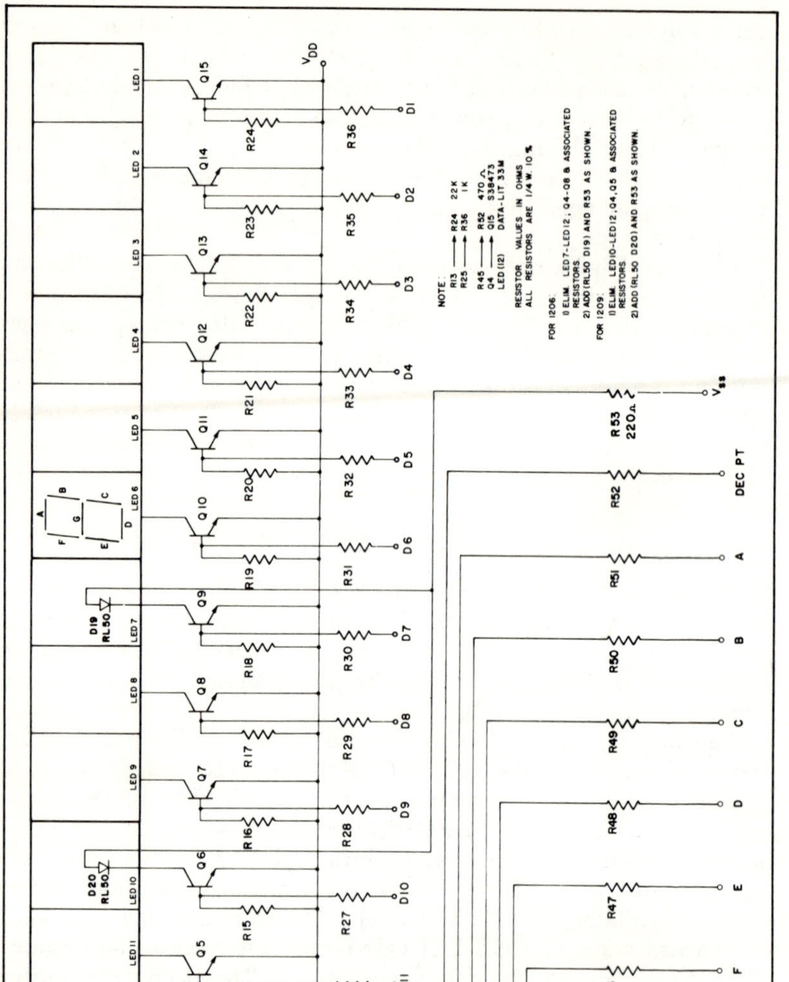

Fig. 6-3. MITS 1200 calculator display schematic.

Fig. 6-4. LED segment driver.

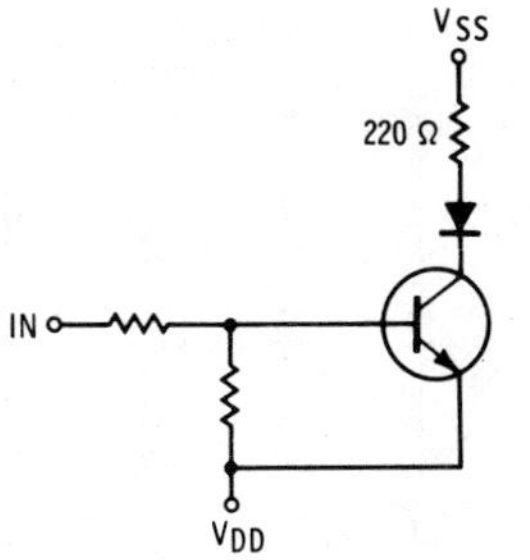

The display circuit of the MITS Model 1200 calculator drops approximately 0.5 volts across the transistor, 5.3 volts across the series resistor, and 1.7 volts across the LED. From Ohm's law, this gives a peak current of about 24 mA through the LED junction. Since there are 12 digits in the calculator, each display in the readout has a duty cycle (total *on* time) of 1/12 or 0.083. This gives an average current consumption of only 2 mA. If all seven segments and the decimal point of a single display unit are activated simultaneously to form the digit 8, then the total current drain at 2 mA per segment is 16 mA. Therefore, a 12-digit display in which all segments and a single display are illuminated would consume some 170 mA of average current. Normally much less than 60% of the segments in a display are on at any one time; for example, the average total current consumption of the calculator is under 25 mA.

The operating parameters of the LED readout used in the MITS Model 1200 series calculators are similar to those of other miniature calculators employing an LED readout. Since the current consumption of an LED readout is much higher than that of the remainder of the calculator, the 1200 machines and several other calculators employ an automatic display blanking circuit. This circuit initiates a timing sequence with each keyboard entry. When sufficient time has elapsed from the last entry, the display is automatically deactivated to conserve battery life. Previous numerical and function entries are unaffected by the blanking circuit, and the display can be reactivated by simply pressing the = key or making a new numerical entry. The delay before the display is deactivated ranges from about 15 seconds to a full minute, with different manufacturers offering different delays.

Thus far we have described the operation of a single LED segment of a seven-segment display. Fig. 6-5 shows how all seven segments and the decimal point are connected within a display unit. Notice that all the anodes of each segment and the decimal point are all connected. This arrangement permits the desired segments to be illuminated with a single input to each segment.

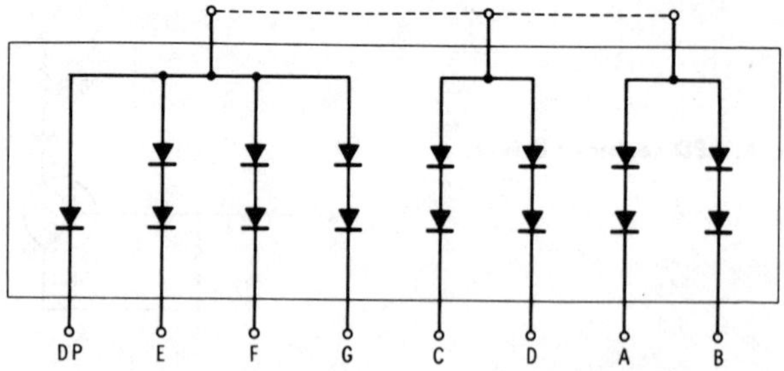

Fig. 6-5. LED display equivalent circuit.

Fig. 6-3 shows how twelve 7-segment displays in a Model 1200 calculator are connected. Transistors Q4 through Q15 are the digit enable drivers (sometimes called digit strobe drivers). Normally all the display units are off, but an input signal to the base of one of the drive transistors will activate its respective display unit.

The operation of the multiplexing can be best understood by examining a single display unit and its drive circuitry. Consider the first display unit (LED 12) in Fig. 6-3. When the calculator is in operation, all segments of LED 12 are potentially on since all the display units are connected in parallel. When a positive input signal is applied to the base of Q4, Q4 turns on and activates LED 12. The LED then displays the digit being simultaneously sent to all 12 display units. Of course the remaining 11 units are off, and the displays are sequenced on and off so rapidly that they appear to be on continuously.

The total peak current at this point can be quite high if all seven segments and the decimal point are activated. Since the peak current through each segment in a typical display is 24 mA, the total peak current will be 192 mA when all segments and the decimal point are illuminated. Since conventional MOS integrated circuits normally cannot withstand this much current, external strobing transistors are almost always used in miniature calculators with an LED display. Due to the current sensitivity of MOS calculator chips, a calculator which shows evidence of defective multiplex circuitry (missing display segments, etc.) should not be operated until the problem has been isolated and repaired.

Fig. 6-3 shows two resistors associated with each of the 12 strobing transistors Q4 through Q15. To see how the values of these resistors are determined, consider transistor Q4 and its resistors, R13 and R25. Resistor R25 is selected first, and since Q4 must switch a maximum of 192 mA, its current gain (HFE) must be considered in the selection of R25. The MITS 1200 calculator employs strobe driver transistors having a minimum HFE of about 50. Therefore, in order for Q4 to switch 50 mA an input signal of 1 mA is required. To obtain the maximum required value of 192 mA, Q4 will require an input signal of about 3.84 mA $(192 \div 50 = 3.84)$. Now it is a simple matter to determine the resistance of R25. Transistor Q4 will have a voltage drop of about 0.7 volts when it is conducting. Since the power-supply voltage in this case is 7.5 volts, R25 must drop 6.8 volts. To determine the value of R25, Ohm's law is invoked and the voltage across R25 is divided by the current required to switch 192 mA through Q4. The result is 1770 ohms $(6.8 \div 0.00384 = 1770.8)$. To be certain that the display of the Model 1200 calculator will operate reliably, R25 and the remaining input limiting resistors are only 1000 ohms. This is significantly less than the required 1770 ohms, but the lower value ensures proper operation of the display when the battery voltage has dropped below its normal value.

Resistor R13 and the other resistors connected from the base of each strobe driver to a common line prevent the transistors from turning on due to leakage currents which may be present in the circuit. If a transistor begins to turn on due to leakage current, the display may exhibit *afterglow*, an effect characterized by the partial illumination (when they should be completely off) of some segments of one or more display units. Afterglow can be undesirable if the leakage currents are high enough.

So long as R13 through R24 are below 50,000 ohms each, the strobe driver transistors will not permit enough leakage current to cause afterglow. In fact, these resistors can even be removed from the circuit shown in Fig. 6-3 with only a dim red glow appearing on all segments of each display unit. The glow is a result of the very small leakage currents through Q4 through Q15 and is so dim it can be seen only when viewed in subdued ambient light.

ELECTROFLUORESCENT DISPLAYS

The electrofluorescent display provides one of the most attractive and legible readout devices presently available. Due to their relatively high voltage requirement (25 volts), they are used in but a few miniature calculators. But they are very popular in desk machines.

A typical calculator which uses electrofluorescent display tubes is the MITS Model 816, a four-function desk unit. Unlike the single-chip Model 1200 calculator described in the previous sec-

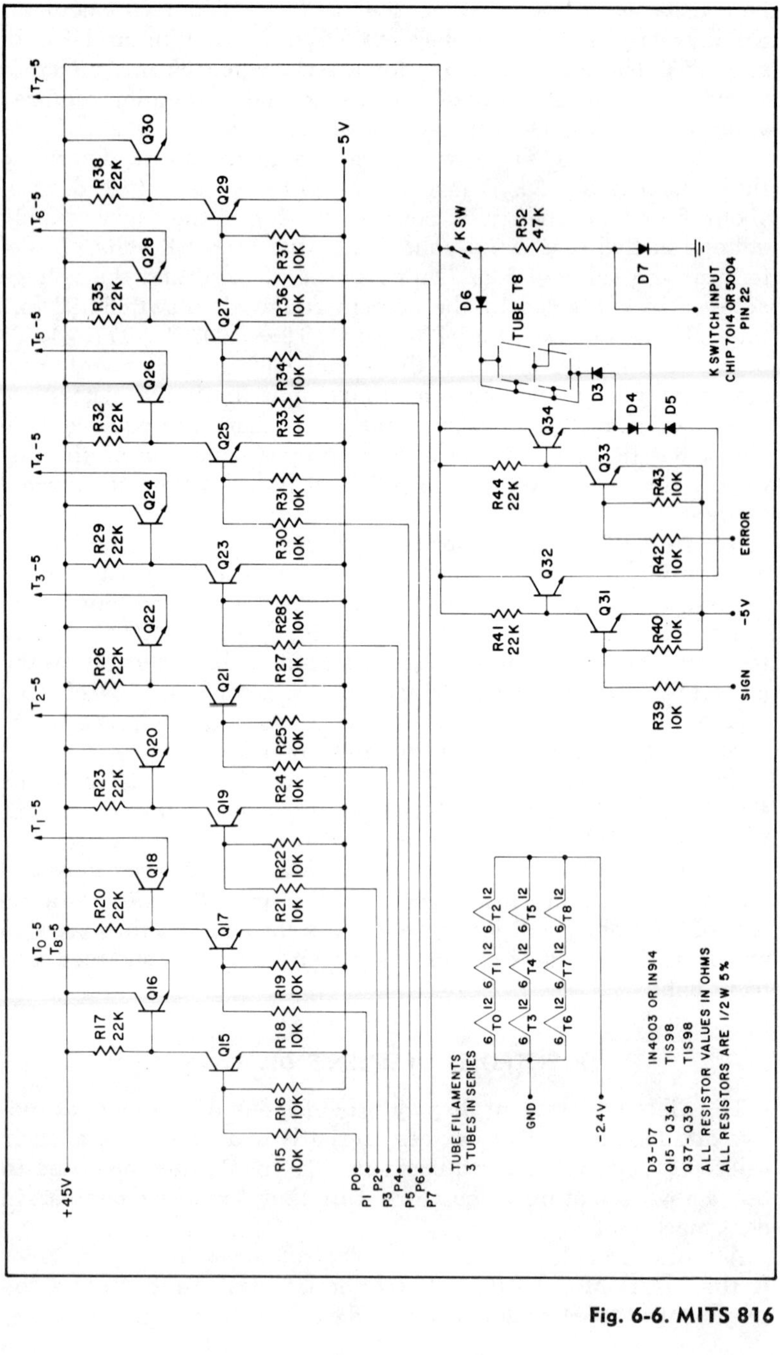

Fig. 6-6. MITS 816

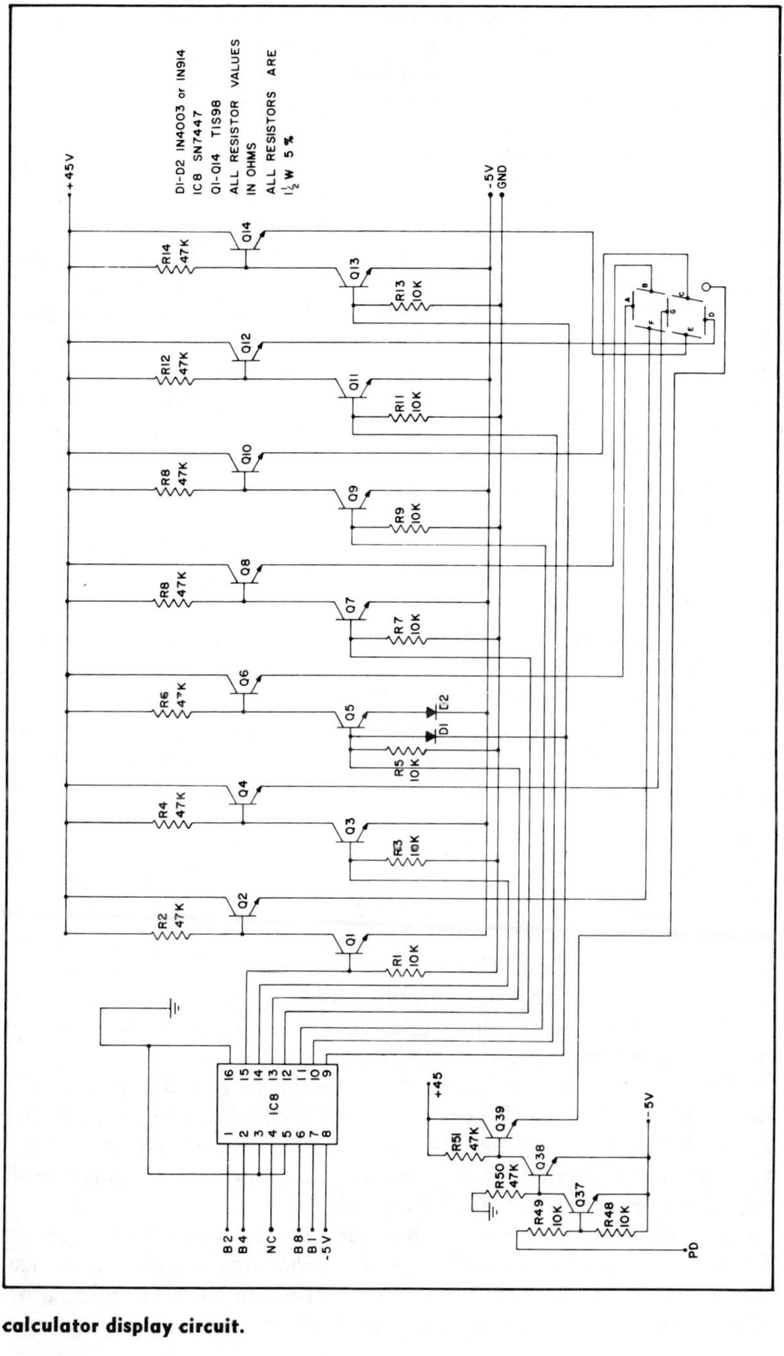

calculator display circuit.

tion on LEDs, the calculator chip set used in the 816 does not incorporate integral BCD to seven-segment display logic. Instead, a separate 7447 decoder IC is employed to convert the BCD output of the calculator chips into a digital format.

Fig. 6-6 shows the display circuitry of the 816 in detail. The 7447 decoder is labelled IC6 in the schematic. Since the 7447 has insufficient power for adequately driving the segments directly, separate transistors Q1 through Q14 are utilized for this purpose. Note that two transistors are required for each segment. This is because the 7447 produces a low output when it activates a segment. In practice, the most positive output of the 7447 is ground while the most negative output is minus five volts. (These are not typical TTL signal levels.) When the negative output is applied to Q1, for example, Q1 turns off. This causes Q2, which is connected as an emitter follower, to conduct and apply a large positive voltage to its segment, in this case segment F.

The combinations of Q1 and Q2, Q3 and Q4, etc. are called a *buffer stage*. In the 816, the buffer stages switch approximately 45 volts to the appropriate segments when enabled by the 7447 output lines. Other calculators employing electrofluorescent displays may use slightly different voltage levels.

The display of the 816 calculator is multiplexed by means of strobe driver transistors Q15 through Q29 in the lower portion of the circuit diagram in Fig. 6-6. All the display tubes receive the same BCD signal simultaneously since all their segments are connected in parallel. Each tube is normally off, however, and the strobe drivers sequentially activate each of the tubes one after another.

The strobe driver for display tube T_1 consists of Q17 and Q18 (see Fig. 6-6). A positive signal is necessary to activate the display tube, and this is why two transistors are required for each driver. In the case of the 816, a signal at line P1 goes negative when it selects a digit. This causes Q17 to turn off which, in turn, causes Q18 to conduct and supply a positive 45-volt signal to the control grid of the display tube. As in the case of the segment drivers, Q18 forms an emitter follower.

The circuitry in the lower right portion of Fig. 6-6 (Q31, Q32, Q33, Q34) forms the decimal point driver and the error tube, T8. In the 816, the error tube displays a minus sign if required and a *C* when the CONSTANT switch is set. The tube also displays an *E* when an error in data entry has occurred.

The selection of resistors for the display tube and segment drivers in the 816 is similar to the procedure employed in the design of the LED display of the MITS Model 1200 calculator. The minimum current gain of the drive transistor and the current requirement of the display are determined, and the resistor values are selected accordingly.

OTHER DISPLAYS

Several other seven-segment display devices are used in modern calculators, notably gaseous glow-discharge tubes and liquid-crystal displays. The driving and multiplexing schemes employed with these machines are similar in principle to those described thus far with several major exceptions. Glow-discharge tubes, for example, require a much higher operating voltage (200 volts), and therefore buffer circuitry must be designed with care.

Liquid-crystal displays are advantaged by an extremely low power and moderate voltage requirement, but their very slow response time complicates the design of multiplexing circuitry. Until recently, liquid-crystal displays were driven in the conventional, nonmultiplexed mode with a separate decoder/driver for each digit. Several novel time-sharing circuits have been designed which permit even liquid-crystal displays to be multiplexed.

TROUBLESHOOTING DISPLAY CIRCUITS

Though the display circuit is the most complex part of most calculators, excluding the calculator chips themselves, it can be the easiest circuitry to troubleshoot. In fact, a good technician can frequently isolate a defective transistor in the display circuit without using a single piece of test equipment. He simply observes the display in operation and follows the general guidelines given below.

If a single display unit is inoperative but the remaining digits in the display operate normally, the calculator central processing circuitry is good. Also, the segment drivers and decoder(s) are operating normally since all remaining digits, which share common multiplexing circuitry, appear normal. Since only a single digit is bad, either its strobe driver transistor is defective or the digit itself is inoperative. Some display devices do become completely inoperative, particularly gaseous-discharge and electrofluorescent devices. In both cases a cracked envelope will render the display inoperative. In the case of the electrofluorescent device, a broken filament will extinguish the display. Light emitting diode displays rarely become completely bad all at once since each segment is an independent light source. Instead, one or perhaps two segments may become defective.

Sometimes a defective calculator MOS chip will cause a blank digit by not providing the proper drive signal at the appropriate time, but this would be unusual since a defective chip usually causes more than one digit to fail. In fact, the MOS output chip should be suspected if more than one digit is blank. An oscilloscope can be used to check if the MOS chip is supplying digit drive signals.

A relatively simple troubleshooting problem is a single defective segment in an otherwise properly operating display. Since all respective segments in each digit are connected together, a simple defective segment almost always indicates either a bad solder connection at the display or a defective display device. If the segment fails to light after resoldering the suspect connection(s), the display itself is defective and should be replaced.

Another basic problem occurs when the same segment in all display devices is out. If the remainder of the display is working normally, the problem is almost always due to a defective segment-driver transistor or a bad solder connection between the driver and the display. If the circuit does not employ segment-driver transistors, the problem can usually be traced to a bad connection. A defective decoder can also cause the problem, but usually a bad decoder causes more display problems than simply a single missing segment.

The most difficult display problem is a failure of the entire display. The most likely cause is a power-supply problem, so it is important to make sure the display is receiving proper voltage before initiating the troubleshooting procedure. If the power supply is operating properly and connections from the power supply to the display are good, the most likely source of the trouble is the decoder IC. Of course, all the segment and digit drivers could be defective, but such a simultaneous failure is highly unlikely. If the decoder is working properly, the calculator chip(s) itself may be defective. The central processing circuitry may not be supplying drive signals to the decoder, thus the display is blanked for lack of enabling signals.

There are several other types of display problems, and most can be approached in the same manner as those described thus far. Calculator troubleshooting is discussed in more detail in Chapter 10.

CHAPTER 7

Calculator Printers

Many calculator applications require a permanent record of entries, calculations, and results. "Hard-copy" printers are more complex than visible displays, but recent technological developments have simplified several classes of printing devices.

This chapter describes three important classes of hard-copy printers suitable for use with calculators: mechanical impact, electrostatic, and semiconductor thermal printers. There are other important printing devices, but those described here are representative of most devices in current or projected use.

IMPACT PRINTERS

Most printing calculators in production today utilize mechanical impact-type printers such as the one shown in Fig. 7-1. While the rapid development of newer and quieter printing technologies is making an important contribution to the design of new printing calculators, impact printers will likely be incorporated in calculators for some time to come.

A typical impact printer of the type used in electronic calculators is the Model 55 Parallel Printer made by the Addmaster Corporation. This unit is a 12-column scanning printer capable of printing up to three lines (36 characters) per second. Each of the 12 print wheels can contain up to 12 characters. The standard configuration is a blank, a decimal, and the digits 0 through 9, though the manufacturer will supply other character arrangements on special order.

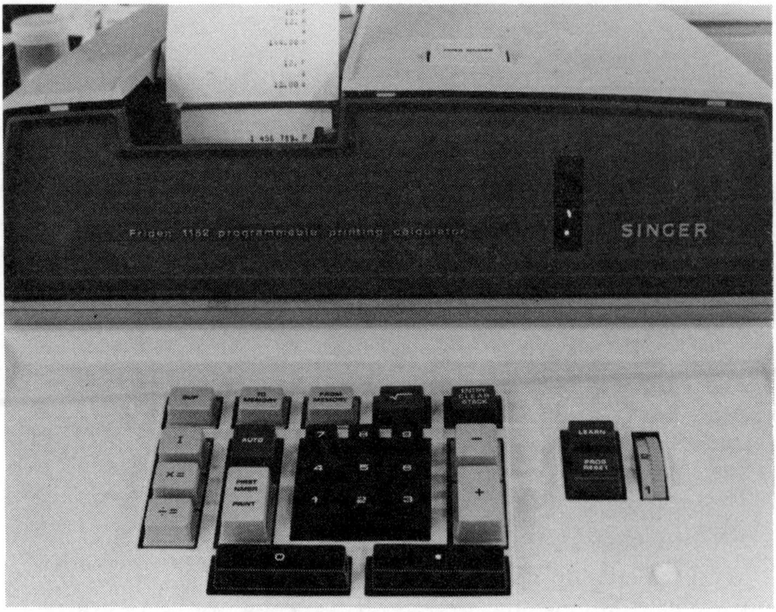

Fig. 7-1. The Friden 1152 calculator employing electromechanical printer.

The Addmaster Model 55 illustrates several important advantages of impact printers over newer printing technologies. The device is completely self-contained, uses standard adding-machine paper, and prints a full line of characters simultaneously. Of even more significance, the printed output is highly legible and can be obtained in a variety of colors. Printers employing electrostatic or thermal techniques do not produce the highly legible print of impact printers.

While impact printers are desirable for their output format and ability to use standard, readily available paper, they possess several distinct disadvantages. Perhaps the major problem is noise. As their name implies, impact printers transfer an inked impression of a raised character by means of an electromechanically driven hammer. Depending upon the design of the printer, one or more print hammers may be used, and the result is high operating noise. The noise from printing calculators which use an impact printer can be bothersome in a crowded office, and their use is completely prohibited in areas such as libraries and study rooms.

Another major disadvantage of impact printers is their size and weight. The Addmaster Model 55, for example, is considered a compact printer, yet it occupies a volume measuring 5½″ × 10″ ×

8″ and weighs 5½ pounds. These dimensions exceed those of a stack of half a dozen pocket calculators.

Despite their disadvantages, impact printers represent the best of all calculator printing devices. Numerous variations in mechanical construction exist, but most produce high-quality copy and are highly reliable. Nevertheless, as improvements in technology continue, it is likely that traditional mechanical printers will be ultimately replaced by quieter, more efficient techniques.

ELECTROSTATIC PRINTERS

An important new class of nonimpact printing devices is the electrostatic printer such as the PR1001 of Elec-Trol, Inc. This device incorporates an electrosensitive paper divided into columns. The device is capable of printing in a 7 × 9 or 5 × 7 dot-matrix format in each column. (The 7 × 9 characters measure 13 × 10 mils.)

The obvious advantage of the PR1001 over most impact printers is its alphanumeric capability. Due to size limitation, most impact printers are limited to the ten digits and perhaps a few symbols. With a suitable character generator ROM, the PR1001 will print the entire 96-character ASCII code. The unit even prints both upper and lower case alphabetic characters. Since no print hammers are employed, the unit is significantly quieter than impact printers.

Though electrostatic printers offer important advantages over traditional impact printers, they are disadvantaged by their requirement of special printing tape and the newness of their technology. Nevertheless, several calculator manufacturers have already successfully incorporated electrostatic printers into their products.

THERMAL PRINTERS

Currently most electronic calculators employ electromechanical printers, but newly developed semiconductor thermal printers will almost certainly change this situation in the near future. Electromechanical printers are generally noisy, but operation of the thermal printer is nearly silent.

Thermal printers, as the name implies, form characters on heat-sensitive thermographic paper. The thermal printhead consists of an array of semiconductor "heaters" which can be activated to form alphanumeric characters in a dot or bar format. Fig. 7-2 shows a typical printhead configuration. There are several types of thermal printers, but most employ either a monolithic silicon

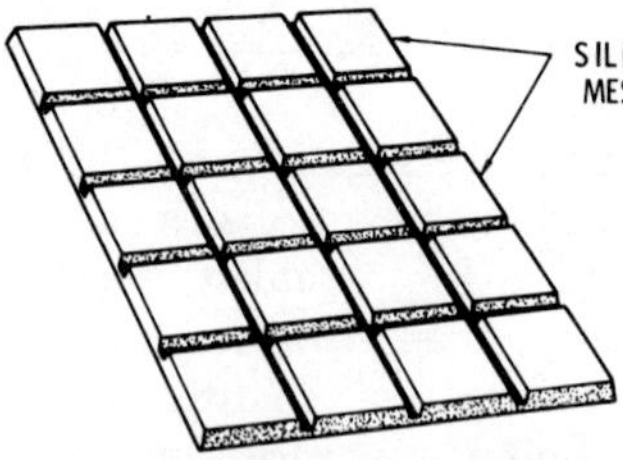

Fig. 7-2. Thermal printhead array.

structure or an array of thin-film resistors made of a resistive substance such as tin oxide. Another approach utilizes an array of thick-film resistors. Fig. 7-3 shows how a thermal printhead is used in an operational printer.

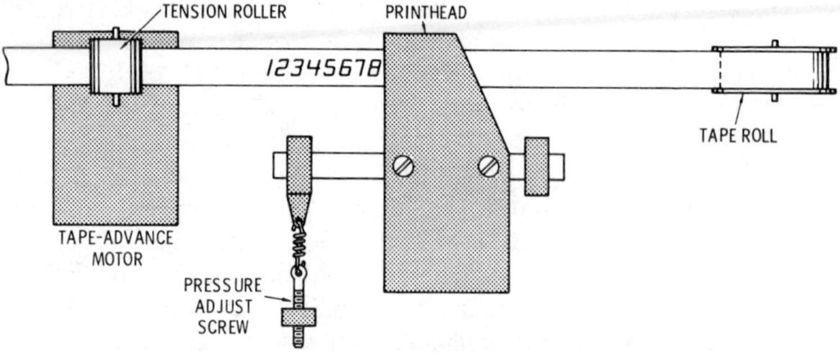

Fig. 7-3. Typical thermal printer mechanical configuration.

Texas Instruments, a pioneer in the development of light emitting diode displays, was one of the first firms to manufacture and market a successful thermal printhead, and the new device found immediate use in the Canon Pocketronic portable calculator (Fig. 7-4). Because of the relatively large size of the Pocketronic's total printing mechanism, which includes an advancement device, a mechanical chassis, and a reel of paper tape, the machine is not really in the "pocket" category. Nevertheless, the introduction of the Pocketronic represented a major development in the field of miniature printing calculators.

Because many people who work with numbers require a permanent record of their calculations and because calculators with a noisy electromechanical printer are unpopular in a crowded office, the Pocketronic initially enjoyed a good commercial reception. However, the ticker-tape style output of the device (a ¼-inch paper type) was expensive and inconvenient for permanent record keeping and even checking past calculations several inches down the tape. For this reason, calculator manufacturers, including Canon, have shifted their design efforts away from the single-character thermal printer with ticker-tape output to printers capable of producing the same line-by-line format as the conventional adding machine.

The Pocketronic used the original Texas Instruments thermal printhead with a 4 × 5 dot matrix array. Newer machines use linear arrays of thermal printhead on a common substrate. One

Fig. 7-4. The Canon Pocketronic calculator employes thermal printer and ticker-tape-style readout.

example is the nine-character unit made by Displaytek. This palm-sized printer weighs only eight ounces with a 100-foot roll of paper tape, prints in the adding-machine format, and uses a single solenoid to advance the tape. This printer incorporates nine 7-segment semiconductor thermal printheads on a 175- × 460-mil monolithic chip. The rectangular chip is bonded to a board with the required number of printed-circuit input terminals.

Displaytek also manufactures a 5 × 7 dot matrix thermal printhead. This device is in the form of a 150- × 150-mil chip containing some 200 separate components, including driver transistors. Like the seven-segment array printhead, the dot matrix chip uses the latest in electrode connection technology and beam leads, and it has internal temperature compensation. The latter feature regulates the temperature of the printhead, which would otherwise vary with ambient temperature, to give an output with a consistent, uniform appearance. Because of the temperature-regulation feature, the Displaytek printheads require no metal heat sink.

Texas Instruments is not easily giving up its pioneering role in the development of thermal printers. One major calculator manufacturer is exploring the use of a mechanically slewed Texas Instruments thermal printer to produce an adding-machine format with a single printing element.

The firm has also taken what may at first seem a backward step in removing the integrated driver circuitry from the printhead, but actually the result is more economy and longer lifetime. Texas Instruments claims an increase of printhead life of fifty times over earlier versions, giving an incredible 50-million-character print capability.

Besides reducing cost and increasing lifetime, Texas Instruments continues to introduce new printers. Because of the silent, solid-state operation of its printers, the company has found a ready acceptance of them by the military, and one result is a 25-characters-per-line printer developed for the Air Force which prints 300 lines per minute.

Thermal printers are not only quieter than electromechanical versions, but they have a much longer operating lifetime as well. If a typical calculation requires, say, ten lines of print, a 50-million-character printer would have a predicted mean lifetime of some 5 million calculations. It is safe to say that most calculator users would require only a fraction of that capability over the usable life of the machine.

Though thermal printers are quiet and long lived, they suffer from several disadvantages. From the manufacturer's viewpoint, user acceptance is one of the biggest drawbacks. Thermal printer manufacturers report calculator companies are reluctant to invest capital and time in a relatively new device when electromechanical printers have already proved their reliability.

From a more practical standpoint, thermal printers do not produce the highly legible and readable copy of most electromechanical units and they lack the ability to produce multiple copies. The former problem is a result of the seven-segment array or dot matrix format of the printhead and seems to be unavoidable. The problem of multiple copies is being attacked by the National Cash Register Company, a potential major user of thermal printers, and one result is a two-layer, chemically impregnated paper tape which, in conjunction with a higher printhead temperature, produces two copies.

Still another disadvantage of thermal printers is the higher cost of the special heat-sensitive paper they require. Electromechanical printers will print on conventional paper tape.

Despite their inherent disadvantages, thermal printers appear to be here to stay. They are lightweight, compact, nearly silent in operation, and competitively priced with electromechanical devices.

THERMAL PRINTER OPERATION

Since thermal printers are sure to capture a wide share of the printer market, it is important to consider the operating characteristics and requirements of typical devices. For this discussion we will first describe the Texas Instruments EPN2100 thermal printer and then several Displaytek units.

The Texas Instruments EPN2100 incorporates an array of 20 silicon mesas in a 4 × 5 format. Each mesa measures 13 × 17 mils and all are thermally isolated, defined dot patterns. Poor isolation produces undesirable fuzziness which hinders legibility.

Electrical connections to the silicon mesas are made by means of a metallic pattern between the mesas and a ceramic substrate. The substrate incorporates a second metalized pattern to which electrical input connections are made. In the case of the EPN2100, a flat, Mylar-encased multilead cable is soldered to the ceramic connections. Assembly of the thermal printhead is completed by attaching the ceramic substrate to an aluminum heat sink.

Each silicon mesa of the EPN2100 is capable of producing a maximum temperature of 250°C within 12 milliseconds of an applied current pulse. Thermographic paper held in contact with the printhead at 10 psi by means of a felt pressure pad will reach a temperature of 200°C when the printhead mesas are at their maximum of 250°C. Since the darkening threshold for conven-

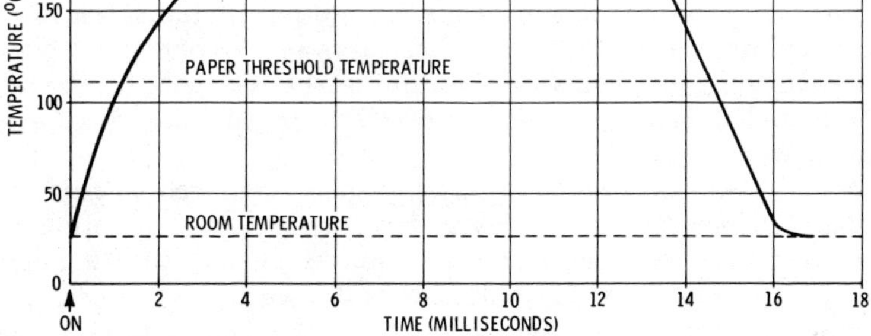

Fig. 7-5. EPN 2100 thermal printhead temperature cycle.

tional thermographic paper is about 110°C, the thermal printhead produces more than enough heat energy. Fig. 7-5 sums up the temperature characteristics of the EPN2100.

Like other Texas Instruments thermal printheads, the EPN2100 achieves heating by means of a transistor-resistor pair contained within each silicon mesa. Fig. 7-6 shows the equivalent circuit used for the EPN2100. The resistor acts as the heating element, while the transistor serves as a current switch to activate the resistor. In a typical application, the resistor is connected to a positive source of about 15 volts. The resistor is connected to the collector of the npn transistor internally, and the emitter of the transistor is brought out to ground. The mesa is energized by means of an input signal at the base of the transistor.

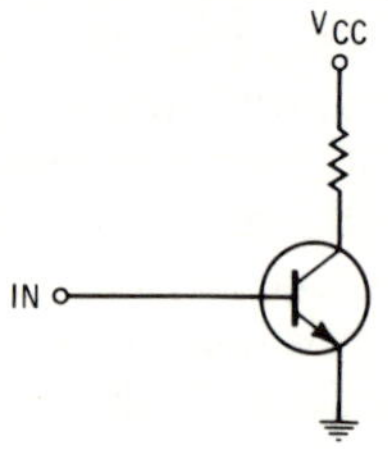

Fig. 7-6. Equivalent circuit for single heating element of EPN 2100.

Texas Instruments recommends that the EPN2100 be multiplexed for most efficient operation. In this operating mode the five rows of mesas are energized sequentially in a time-sharing manner. Besides simplifying external decoding logic, multiplexing reduces peak driving current over what would be required if all rows were activated simultaneously. Since each row contains four mesas and since the maximum current requirement for a single energized mesa is 150 mA, the peak current required for any one row is 600 mA. Operating current, the current level that is sunk after the mesas begin to heat, is even less and is a maximum of 240 mA for a row in which all mesas are activated.

Since only about 60% of the mesas are activated during a single print cycle, the average power consumption of the EPN2100 at its maximum print rate of 9.3 characters per second is 1.4 watts. The heat sink supplied with the printhead must therefore be supplemented in order to keep the temperature of the printer at or below 55°C.

Fig. 7-7 shows the logic timing diagram required to print the letter *E*. Current requirements for the printing operation are shown in Fig. 7-8. A finite time is required between printing operations, in this case 48 milliseconds between characters. This delay time, which corresponds to four of the cycle times required for activating each row, permits the printhead to cool before the

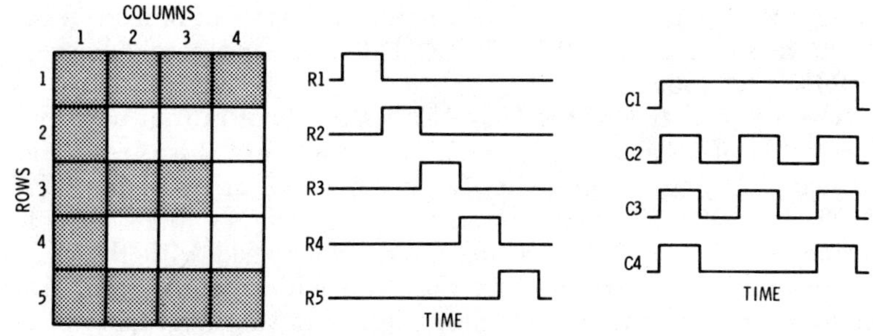

Fig. 7-7. Timing cycle to print letter "E."

next character is printed. Normally the paper tape is moved during the cooling cycle.

Since the EPN2100 and most other thermal printheads are solid-state devices, reliability is high. Problems may occur, however, in the mechanical interface between the printhead and the thermographic paper. In the case of the EPN2100 and several other similar printheads, the paper must be kept absolutely parallel to the front surface of the printhead. The required pressure of the paper against the printhead is about 10 psi. Due to the small size of the printhead, only a few ounces of force are required to achieve this pressure. Texas Instruments recommends a felt pad to achieve the required pressure.

Like Texas Instruments, Displaytek manufactures a variety of thermal printheads. The firm also markets a complete printing unit containing a paper advance mechanism and decoding logic. One of the most popular printheads made by the company is the DC-1157. This device resembles the Texas Instruments EPN2100

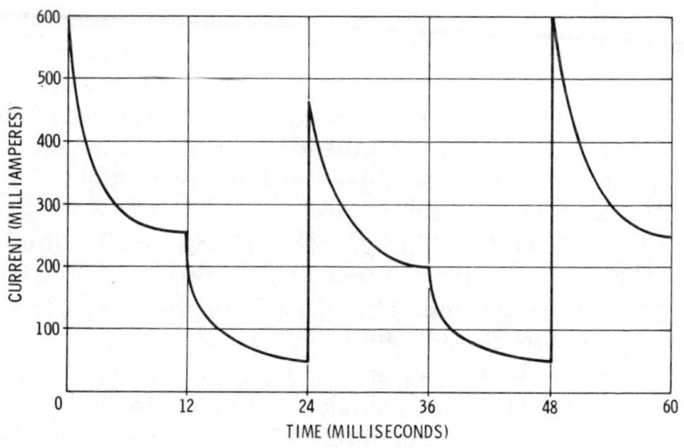

Fig. 7-8. Current cycle to print letter "E."

except that it utilizes a 5 × 7 dot matrix array of silicon mesas. Each mesa measures 9.5 mils × 11.0 mils and total character height is 100 mils.

The 5 × 7 matrix of the DC-1157 is significant in that it permits formation of 96 alphanumeric ASCII characters. Also, resolution and legibility are higher than with the 4 × 5 array of the EPN-2100. The DC-1157 requires an input of from 14 to 18 volts for proper operation. The thermographic paper used with the printhead must be pressed against the head with a pressure of from 20 to 30 psi. The DC-1157 is compatible with thermographic paper made by the 3M Company (Type 161) and NCR (Miniprint Bond). Displaytek has used felt, silicone synthetic rubber, and latex rubber as a pressure pad.

The DC-1157 offers very high printing speeds. Up to 60 characters a second can be printed if a suitable mechanical driving apparatus for the paper is available. Such high printing speeds are made possible by heat buildup within each of the mesas on the printhead. The buildup is not sufficient to blacken the paper on its own, but it does reduce the time constant of the printhead since preliminary heating is provided. At 30 characters per second, for example, a print time of only 6 to 8 milliseconds per character is required.

Another feature of the DC-1157 is an integral temperature-sensing resistor. The resistor permits the printhead temperature to be monitored to correct for variations in the ambient temperature. For example, a thermal printer operated outdoors on a warm day will require less power to achieve paper-blackening threshold than when the same unit is operated in a cold environment. To compensate for ambient temperature changes, the temperature-sensitive resistor can be used to control either the voltage at the printhead or the print time. Either of these steps will permit constant print density.

Besides the DC-1157 described above, Displaytek manufactures a series of segmented thermal printheads. The DC-4180, for example, is a numeric printhead containing from four to sixteen digits assembled in multiples of four. Each digit is a seven-segment array with decimal.

The DC-4180 prints a highly legible character in a line format at from three to six lines per second. The line or adding-machine format is far more convenient and easier to read than the ticker-tape output used with single-head printers.

Several mechanical paper-advance techniques can be employed with thermal printers. Both single- and multiple-character printheads can incorporate a relatively simple solenoid advance mechanism to move the paper character by character or line by line, respectively. An alternate printing arrangement suitable for a full page format is to move a single printhead across the printing paper mechanically. Either constant or interrupted pressure can be applied to the head. The constant-pressure mode is quieter but requires more driving power, while the intermittent mode requires a mechanical interface which will add some noise to the system. When used with nonabrasive thermographic papers, such as 3M's Type 161 or NCR's Miniprint Bond, the wear at the printhead is negligible even when the unit is operated as a page printer in the constant-pressure mode.

CHAPTER 8

Interfacing the Calculator

Because calculators can perform valuable roles as low-cost data processors, this chapter concerns techniques which can be employed to interface the calculator with external devices or systems for data processing. Also presented are methods of interfacing a calculator with additional memory and programming features to convert a basic machine into a more powerful system.

One example of real-time data processing that can be readily performed by a calculator is multiplication of the output from a digital voltmeter by a predetermined constant in order to provide some desired scaling factor. Another example of real-time data processing is an electronic scale in a food market. In this role, the operator feeds in the price per unit weight, and the calculator converts the weight for the quantity of product being purchased into the dollar value that the consumer must pay.

Programming accessories can convert a basic four-function desk machine into a unit with the capabilities of a full computer. When compared to a computer, a fundamental weakness of a desk calculator is speed of operation. However, even though a calculator operates at speeds from ten to a hundred times slower than a computer, this is irrelevant in many applications since calculator speeds are measured in milliseconds or less.

INTERFACING CATEGORIES

Three different types of calculator systems can be obtained with interfacing techniques. In the first technique, which is called an input interface, data is supplied directly to the calculator through the keyboard matrix and then processed (multiplied, divided, etc.) by the calculator. The calculator operates and displays a result just as if the input data had been keyed in by an operator instead of fed directly to the keyboard matrix by electronic means.

In the second interfacing technique, the output of the calculator is used to drive a follow-up system. In a typical application of this technique, an operator inputs a command into a calculator keyboard, and the machine converts the command into a digital signal used to drive some external device.

The third interfacing technique employs auxiliary devices or systems at *both* the input and output of a calculator. One application of this technique is an external programming unit which can either drive or be driven by the calculator itself. This arrangement can be used to provide computer capability in a relatively simple desk-top machine. Fig. 8-1 sums up each of the interface techniques in block diagram form.

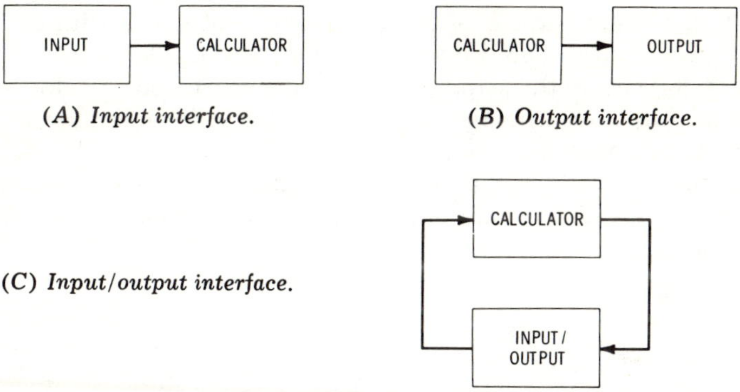

(*A*) *Input interface.*

(*B*) *Output interface.*

(*C*) *Input/output interface.*

Fig. 8-1. Primary interfacing categories.

INPUT INTERFACES

As noted in Chapter 4, the basic input requirement for most MOS calculator chips is a switch closure resistance of less than 100 ohms and an open resistance of greater than 10,000 ohms. These specifications may vary somewhat from manufacturer to manufacturer, but those given here are typical values.

Since the input conditions are not critical, many kinds of electronic switching devices can be used to control the input matrix. Bipolar and field-effect transistors are frequently used as switches, and occasionally light-sensitive phototransistors and photocells are used. Mechanical switches such as relays can be used so long as bounce specifications are not exceeded. In most cases, bounce must not exceed five milliseconds or multiple entries or commands will result. Since many kinds of electromechanical relays exhibit bounce times in excess of 100 milliseconds, suitable care must be exercised in the choice of a switching device.

A TYPICAL INPUT INTERFACE

In this section we will examine a typical function that can be generated using only an input interface. The function, which was developed a few years ago at MITS on an experimental basis, is designed to automatically compute the amount of state sales tax on dollar transactions in a particular state. A MITS customer requested a calculator which would incorporate a special TAX key. When the calculator presented the total amount of a purchase, the operator would simply press the TAX key and the calculator would automatically calculate the tax due. Since the tax in the customer's state was 5%, the calculator required an input interface which multiplied the total by a constant of 0.05.

Fig. 8-2 shows the sequence generator employed to achieve this special function. The circuit, which is actually a single-function, hard-wired program, consists of a four-bit counter, a four-line to sixteen-line converter, and a circuit which provides a suitable relaxation period and enable period for the keyboard and the special TAX key.

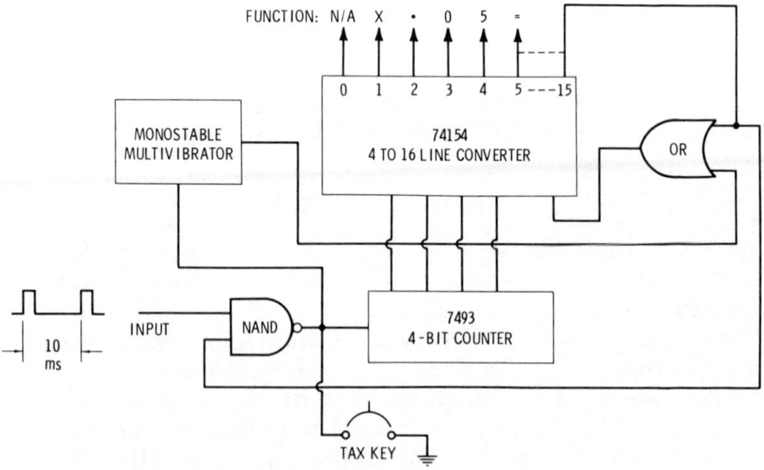

Fig. 8-2. Hard-wired tax calculation sequence generator.

The sequence operates as follows: Assume the counter has reached the binary equivalent of the decimal number 15. This means the last output of the four-line to sixteen-line converter will be *low*. This low signal from the output of the line converter is fed back to the input of the NAND gate where it inhibits clock pulses passing through the gate. With the NAND gate disabled, the sequence generator is inoperable and the calculator operates normally.

Now, assume the TAX key has been pressed. The NAND gate is now opened, and the counter accepts input pulses. The first input pulse advances the line converter to the first output. This output uses no calculator functions, but its activation ensures sequential activation of the remaining outputs from succeeding input pulses. The second pulse activates the second output of the line converter. This output is connected to the MULTIPLY switch position of the calculator keyboard matrix via a transistor or relay switch.

The sequence generator incorporates a monostable multivibrator which limits the line-converter output pulse to a duration of five milliseconds. When this interval has passed, the single shot turns off the decoder, which, in turn, turns off the transistor or relay switch. This permits the keyboard matrix to relax in preparation for the next command, which will occur five milliseconds after the end of the first.

Note that the input clock pulses occur at ten-millisecond intervals. This separation period is essential in meeting the timing requirements for the calculator chip or chips. For example, a typical calculator chip input unit requires an input switch closure of at least five milliseconds and a rest period of also five milliseconds. These specifications ensure that all input commands will be accepted and processed by the input unit. The timing intervals are relatively long in relation to the calculating time of a typical chip, due to the presence of debounce circuitry and provisions for ignoring the second of two nearly simultaneous entries.

Continuing with the operation of the TAX function, the next input pulse steps the line converter to the next output position, which is connected to the DECIMAL switch position of the calculator keyboard matrix via a transistor or relay switch. As with the previous command, the DECIMAL switch is activated for five milliseconds and followed by a five-millisecond relaxation period. The process continues with succeeding input pulses until the following sequence has been activated:

$$(\text{DISPLAY TOTAL}) \times (.05) = \text{TOTAL TAX}$$

The complete timing cycle is shown in Fig. 8-3.

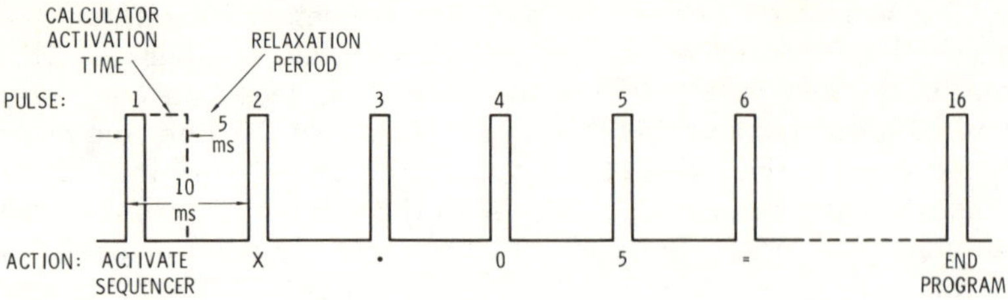

Fig. 8-3. Timing diagram of tax sequence generator.

Note that only seven of the sixteen outputs of the line converter are employed for this special function. After the last active output is reached (*equal*), the counter cycles through the remaining outputs until the last one is reached and the sequence generator is automatically deactivated until the next time TAX is pressed. These additional outputs could be used to implement more complex programs or, as is done here, left unused. For example, two additional outputs could be used to command the calculator to automatically add the tax to the total.

In designing a sequence generator such as this, the engineer must allow additional time for such complex calculation functions as division and square root. Since these and some other functions require far more time for execution than addition and subtraction, an interruption interval must be provided to make sure the calculator has completed the operation before the next key switch is closed.

For example, suppose the special-purpose tax program sequencer described here included a second multiplication command at the output position connected to the EQUAL key. Since multiplication requires from 200 to 500 milliseconds in a typical calculator, input pulses to the four-bit counter would have to be inhibited for at least this period to ensure completion of the multiplication before the next command is generated. Otherwise, the calculator will ignore the next command and simply continue with its computation. The result, of course, is an incomplete program execution.

By incorporating special interrupt intervals into a hard-wired programmer, hundreds of special keyboard functions can be performed by a four-function machine. For a variety of special functions, read-only memories and other techniques can be used.

OTHER INPUT INTERFACES

The special-function technique described in the previous section is useful primarily in applications in which the function does not change. There are many applications and devices, however, which require frequent variation of special functions, and these require a programmable function generator.

One simple programmable function generator is simply a switch matrix which allows the operator to load a new command into the machine following each computation. Due to its cost, this technique is only used when relatively few program steps are required.

A far more versatile programmer employs a RAM or shift-register memory. While this approach permits considerably more programming flexibility than the previous two techniques, it involves a highly complex circuit design. The MITS programmer employs a static RAM, which permits the operator to program up to 512 discrete steps. Because of the random access capability of the RAM, subroutines, unconditional branching, if branching, and other computer-type roles can be readily implemented. These capabilities obviously improve the power of the system over a less sophisticated programming method.

As we noted earlier, some calculator functions take more time to perform than others. It is possible to arrange the timing cycle so that the command intervals exceed the longest possible calculation time, but this is highly inefficient since some operations require as much as half a second, while others are completed in a few milliseconds or less. To minimize delays and ensure the performance of all calculations before new program commands are presented to the calculator (which can be thought of as a data processor when connected to a programmer), a simple technique can be employed. The programmer is connected to the processor input unit where it monitors the operation of the CPU. If a busy signal is present, the programmer pauses; but when no busy signal is present, the programmer steps to the next program instruction. The programmer, therefore, adjusts its operating speed to that of the processor, with a considerable savings in time. For example, discounting the debounce delay time, the MITS 1440 calculator can perform as many as five hundred 14-digit additions a second when connected to a programmer.

It is important to note that this discussion is applicable only to calculators having an *external* programmer. Certain classes of very large programmable calculators, such as the Hewlett-Packard 9820 and 9830, actually incorporate a full digital computer. This, of course, makes the programming and calculator characteristics of the machine indistinguishable. In a machine of this type, both programming and calculation functions employ the same processor, and operations occur in essentially the same manner, whether they are programmed by the user or designed into the machine. While this approach of integrating a digital computer into a programmable calculator provides extensive computing power, it is an exceedingly costly system. In fact, a computer terminal can be leased for less financial outlay than that required for some advanced programmable calculators.

OUTPUT INTERFACING

The programmable sequence generator described earlier in this chapter was limited to an input device. However, this device is far more versatile when it is connected to the output of a calculator; it can accept input information from the machine while simultaneously providing it with inputs.

Unfortunately, interfacing the output of a calculator with a programmer is more difficult than interfacing the input. This is primarily because a complete data word is generated using a parallel-serial scheme, as discussed in Chapter 4. In most cases, interfacing this kind of output data with another device or system requires a timing buffer that detects the start of a data word, loads each digit into an appropriate register, and detects when the complete data word has been loaded. When the data has been completely loaded, the timing buffer must be capable of transferring it to the external device.

INPUT/OUTPUT INTERFACING

The final kind of interfacing is a combination of the input and output types. This interface allows the user to use the calculator processor as an integral data reduction device. It provides a link between data acquisition and final results. For this reason, input/output interfacing is used in sophisticated programmers. The following section will discuss in detail the MITS programmer, which has capabilities between those of medium- and high-powered programmable calculators.

A TYPICAL PROGRAMMER

A programmer with medium- to high-powered capability is a relatively complex device. In order to better understand the various subsystems of such a programmer, the remainder of this chapter will provide a detailed description of the operation of the MITS programmer shown in Fig. 8-4.

The MITS programmer adds 256 programming steps (with the option of expanding to 512 steps) to a MITS 816 or 1440 calculator. The programmer serves as a storage location for extremely long or often used calculator operations. The user can store and run at his convenience such items as long algorithms for trigonometric functions, logarithms, and other complex functions. Instead of entering over and over in the calculator a formula in which only certain variables change, the formula can be entered in the programmer once and then run at will by simply selecting the address where the formula begins and pressing the R (continue) key.

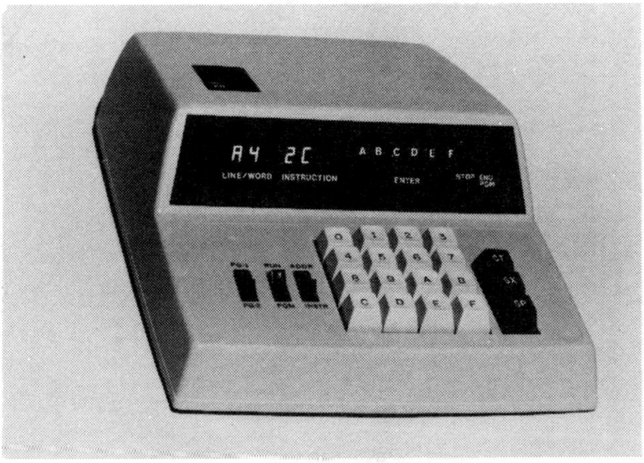

Fig. 8-4. The MITS programmer, an auxiliary device containing 256 or 512 programming steps which can be connected to existing calculators made by MITS.

The programmer automatically executes all steps of the program until it sees a location within the formula where a variable is to be entered. It then temporarily halts execution. When the variable is entered into the calculator, the continue key is pressed again and all remaining steps of the formula are executed until the programmer sees another variable entry or an "End of Program" command.

Each key of the two calculators (816 and 1440) is represented by a special alphanumeric programmer code. The code is entered into the programmer by pressing the appropriate programmer keys associated with each code. Once a complete program has been entered, the user can return to the initial address and either run the program from start to finish, or "step" through each instruction, executing each one at a time.

The MITS programmer has eight basic circuits: *keyboard* and *encoder, mode select, address buffers* (*line* and *word*), *RAM plane, decoder* and *interface, sequence generator, trigger genera-*

tor, and *display*. Fig. 8-5 shows the interrelationship of each of these circuits.

The keyboard (shown in Fig. 8-6) and the encoder circuit convert the sixteen alphanumeric keys (0 through F) into four binary data lines and a load pulse line. The binary data number

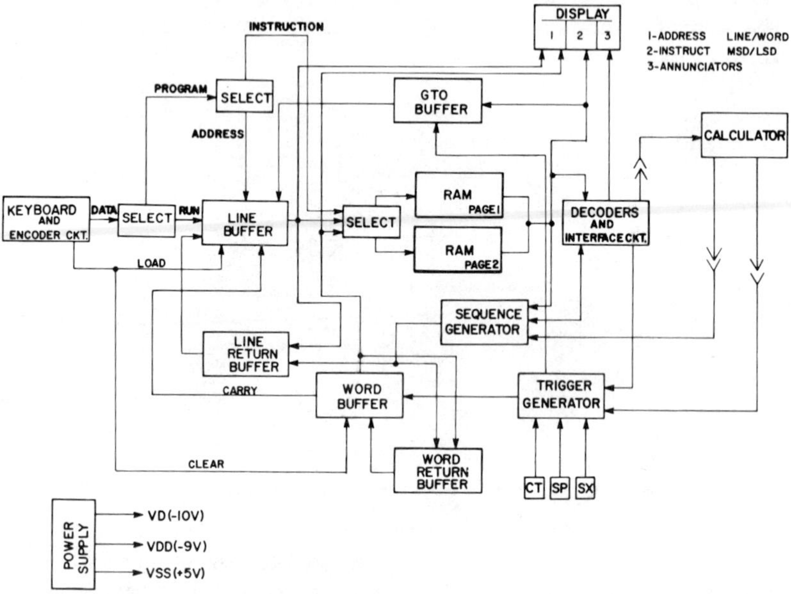

Fig. 8-5. MITS programmer functional diagram.

is then selected, through the RUN/PGM and ADDR/INSTR switches, as either an address or an instruction. An address number is loaded into the address buffer, which goes to the RAM address inputs and selects a location in the RAM. An instruction number goes directly to the RAM data inputs where it is stored in memory.

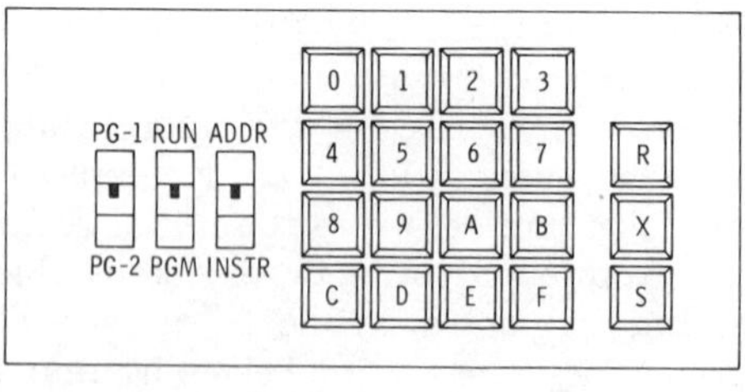

Fig. 8-6. MITS programmer keyboard.

When a RAM location is selected, the data (a seven-bit word) at that location is outputted to the decoder circuit where it is converted to a single line of data and interfaced to the calculator keyboard matrix. The RAM page consists of sixteen lines, each having sixteen words per line and seven bits per word.

The first four bits of the word select the appropriate output of the decoders. The next two bits select one of the decoders, and bit seven enables the sequence generator for internal commands. After a command is given to the calculator, the trigger generator locks out the programmer until the calculator has completed the command. The trigger generator then steps the programmer to the next address in the RAM and halts (if in the step mode) or gives the calculator the next command (if the programmer is in the continue mode).

The display consists of four 7-segment digits and eight indicator status lights. The digits show the address selected in the RAM and the instruction code at that location. The indicator lights (A through F) show the status of the program.

KEYBOARD AND ENCODER CIRCUIT

The keys labeled 0 through 9 and A through F in Fig. 8-6 comprise a four-by-four matrix that detects switch closures. A binary-coded output is produced by the encoder circuit consisting of Q1 through Q3, R6 through R13, and D11 through D14 in Fig. 8-7. For example, pressing the B key (which represents eleven in decimal or 1011 in binary) places a positive voltage at pins 3 and 5 of IC E through D11 and D12, and it also causes Q2 to conduct, which puts a positive voltage at pin 11 of IC E. The following voltage potentials are now found at the inputs of E: pins 1 and 9 are at ground and pins 3, 5, and 11 are positive. Therefore, the decimal number 11 has been encoded to the binary number 1011. The binary lines are inverted at IC E and are then fed to both the line buffer and the RAM data inputs.

Binary lines 1 and 2 and the 0 line (pins 2, 4, and 6 of E) are ORed together to generate the load pulse. The load pulse is fed to the mode select circuit, which loads the binary number into either the address buffer or the RAM, depending upon which mode of operation has been chosen.

MODE SELECT CIRCUIT

This circuit, shown in Fig. 8-8, provides two switches, RUN/PGM and ADDR/INSTR, which select the desired mode of operation. When this circuit is in the program mode, the load pulse is fed to the

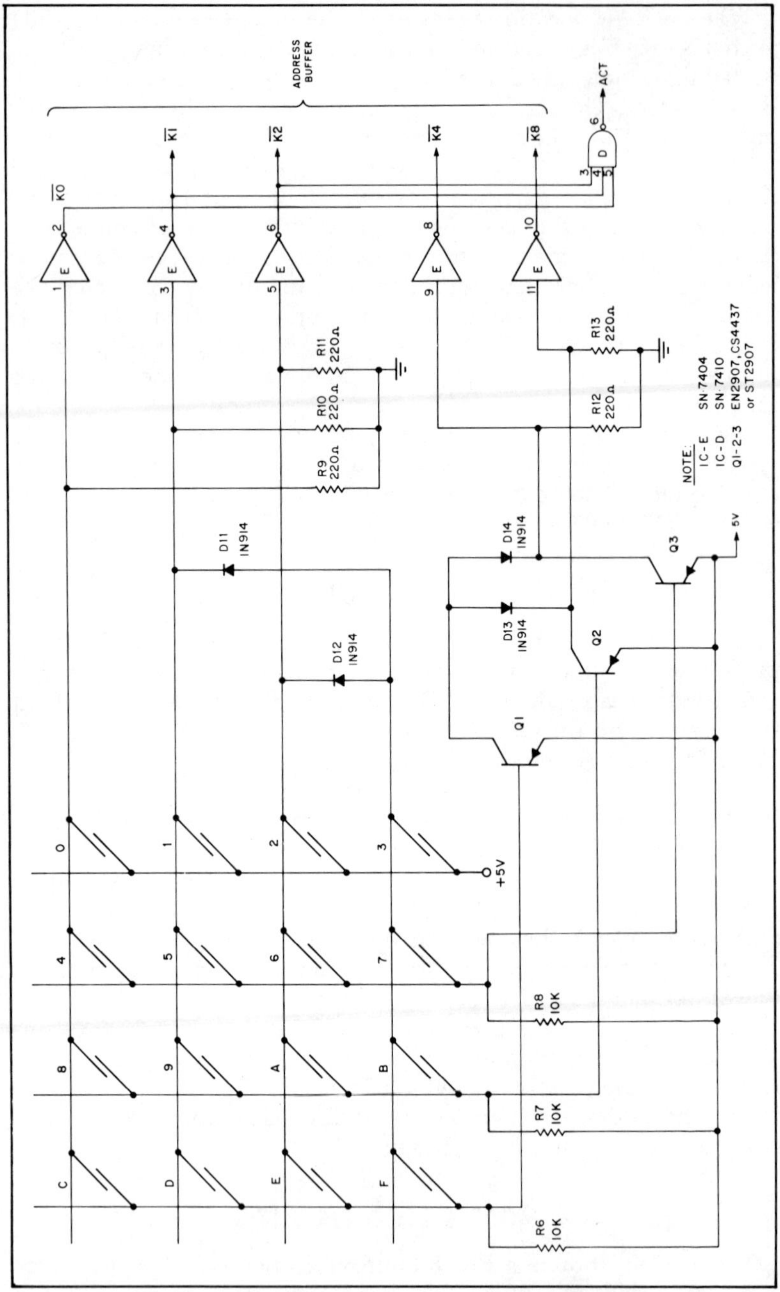

Fig. 8-7. MITS programmer keyboard matrix.

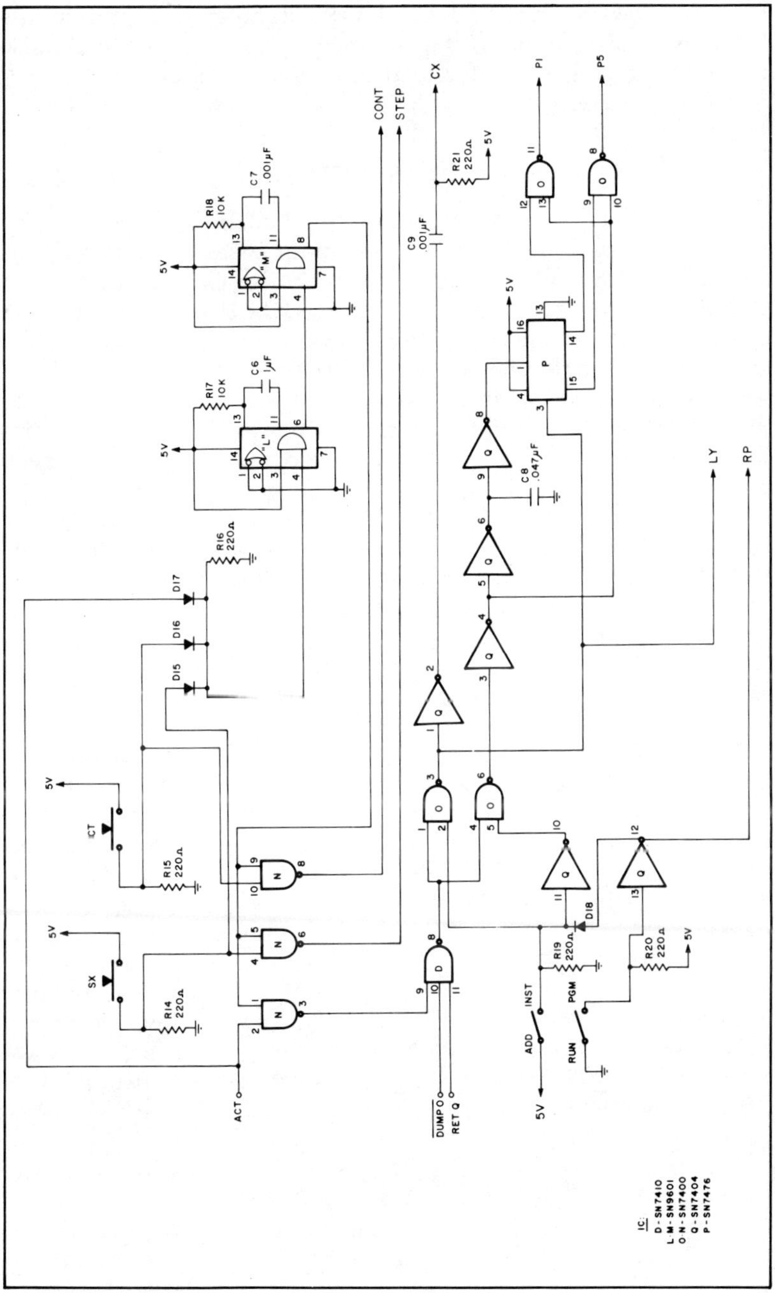

Fig. 8-8. MITS programmer mode-select circuit.

RAM read-write line, and the binary number is stored in the RAM as an instruction. If the run mode is selected, the load pulse is fed to the address buffer load inputs in order to select an address in the RAM page.

ADDRESS BUFFERS

When the load pulse is fed to the line buffer, the four-bit binary number present at the buffer input is stored at its outputs. The load pulse is also fed to the word buffer clear input to reset the word address to zero. These buffers (IC's H and K in Fig. 8-9) are synchronous four-bit binary counters with preset inputs and are connected so that when the word buffer is passing from fifteen (F) to zero, the line buffer is incremented by one. The trigger generator and the x key feed the word buffer load input to increment the word address by one each time an instruction has been executed or the x key is depressed.

The output from the line and word buffers forms an eight-bit binary number. This number is fed to the RAM address inputs in order to select an address in memory. This number is also fed to the line and word digits on the display to give a visual indication of the current address.

RANDOM-ACCESS MEMORY

Each random-access memory (RAM) in the MITS programmer is a 16-pin integrated circuit capable of storing a binary digit at any of 256 different locations within its memory plane. To determine a location for storing one of these digits, an eight-digit binary number is sent to the RAM on the address lines (see Fig. 8-10). This address input is subdivided into line and word inputs, each containing four bits. The first four bits address the line and the last four address the word. For example, binary digits 0010 and 0100 will address line two, word four. This eight-bit input enables the operator to address 16 words per line and 16 lines per RAM page. Fig. 8-11 is a pictorial representation of one page of RAM memory. The MITS programmer comes with a single two hundred fifty-six 7-bit word memory page, which can be expanded to two pages.

The programmer uses seven RAMs, connected as shown in Fig. 8-10, to create a seven-bit output word, the required length for its output data, and internal commands and timing. Each RAM output is one bit of the seven-bit word. The first four RAM outputs are fed to the decoder address inputs in order to select one of sixteen decoder outputs. The next two bits are fed to the de-

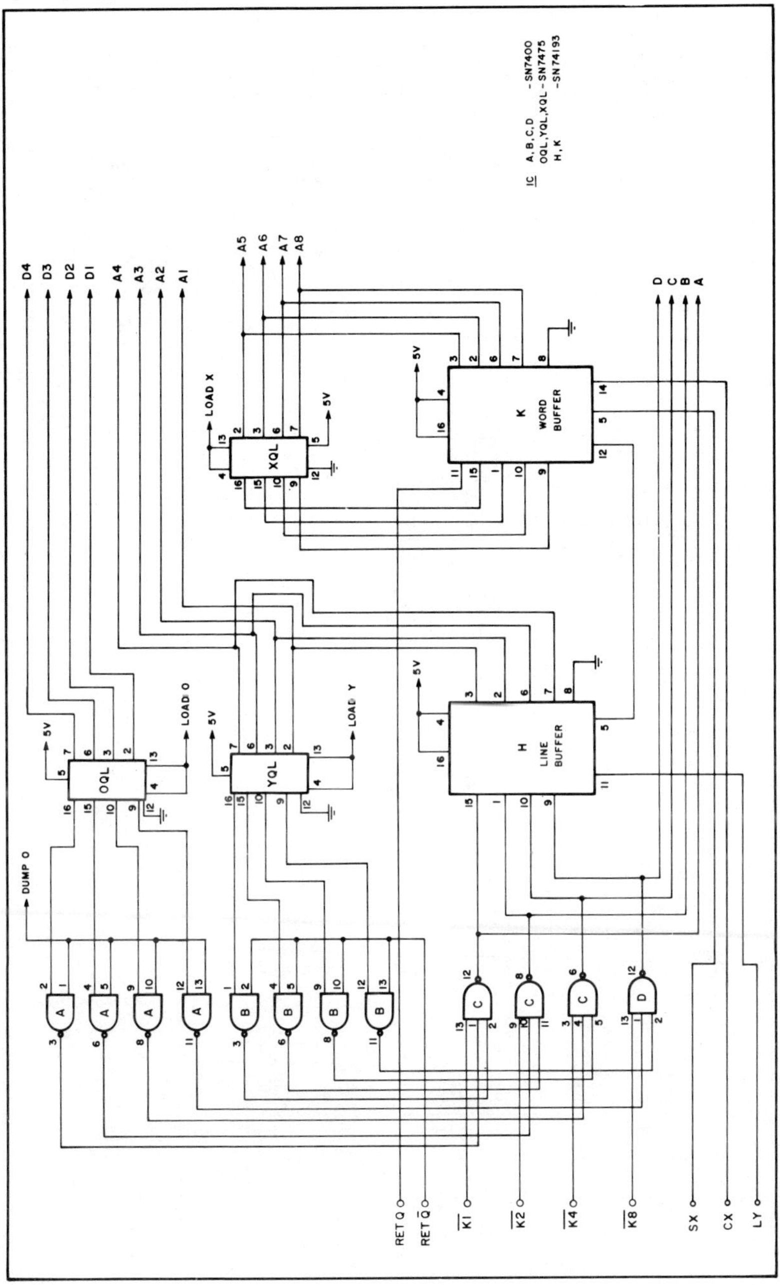

Fig. 8-9. MITS programmer address buffer.

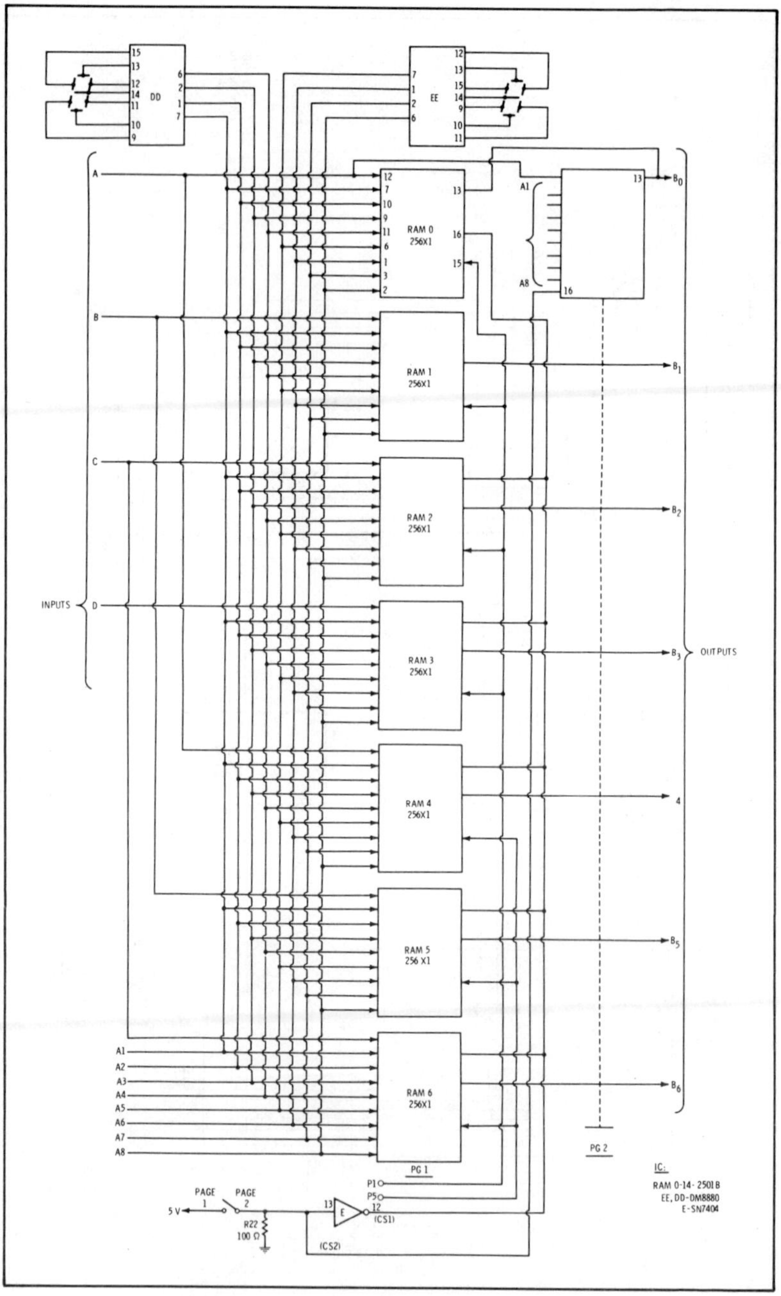

Fig. 8-10. RAM page from MITS programmer.

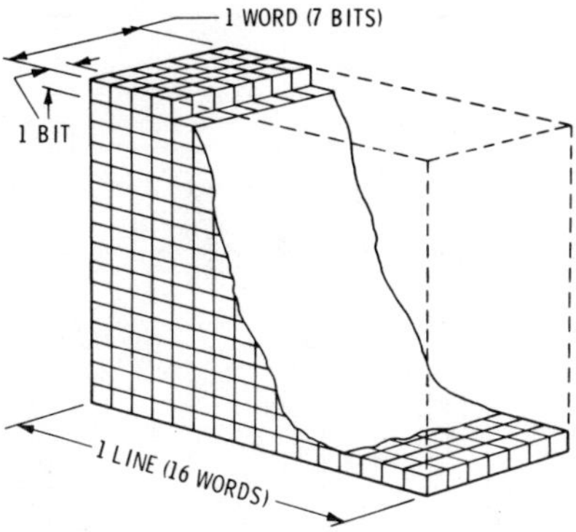

Fig. 8-11. Pictorial representation of RAM memory page.

coder select circuit in order to select one of the three decoders. The same two bits are also fed to the sequence generator circuit in order to partially enable it. The last output, used for selection of special commands, is fed to the sequence generator and decode disable circuit in order to complete the enable circuit for internal commands.

Each RAM has a *data input* and a *read/write input*. The read/write input enables the RAM to either accept information (instruct mode) or output information (address mode). *"Read"* is the address mode of the RAM, and *"write"* is the instruct mode of the RAM. When the read/write input is positive, the information on the RAM data input line is stored in the RAM memory plane. When the read/write input is negative, the data input line is disabled and the information is fed to the RAM address input lines. When the RAM page is addressed, the information within that address is outputted as the seven-bit code. When the programmer is in the PGM mode and a key is depressed, the converted binary number is fed to the RAM data inputs and the load pulse is fed to the read/write inputs. This stores the binary number in the first four RAMs. When a second number is entered, it is stored in the last three RAMs, thus storing a seven-bit word in an address. The seven output lines are also fed to the instruction digits on the display to give a visual indication of the current instruction code at a given address.

DECODER AND INTERFACE CIRCUIT

Bits one through four of the outputted seven-bit instruction are fed to the address inputs of all three of the decoders simultaneously. Each decoder is capable of converting the four input lines of information into any one of sixteen output lines. The decoder and interface circuit, IC's EE and GG in Fig. 8-12, selects the de-

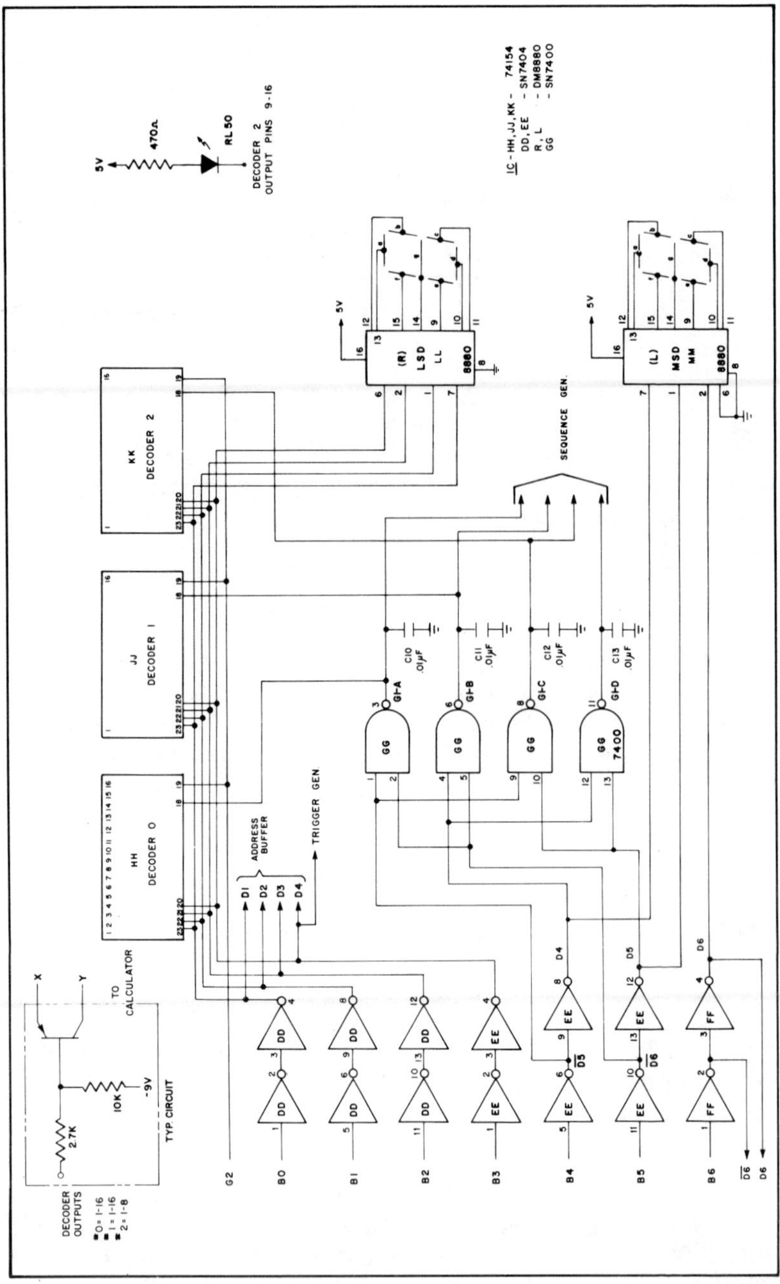

Fig. 8-12. MITS programmer decoder-select circuit.

coder to be enabled in accordance with the information from bits five and six of the instruction word. The correct information is now present at the decoders and one of the three has been selected. The only remaining requirement for a programmer output is a pulse from the trigger generator, which enables input G2 of the decoders. Each active decoder output represents an instruction code, either a calculator command or an internal annunciator (including the stop and EP commands). The outputs representing calculator commands are fed to transistor switches. When these switches are activated, they short the two calculator keyboard matrix lines associated with their particular code. This essentially simulates a calculator key depression and an entry is inputted into the calculator.

TRIGGER GENERATOR

The timing and control for the programmer are provided by the trigger generator circuit shown in Fig. 8-13. Once an initial instruction code has been addressed, this circuit must be activated before the instruction code can be executed. This is done by pressing either the R or X push button on the keyboard. When either of these keys is pressed, IC V generates a pulse to enable the G2 decoder inputs, and this allows the instruction code to be entered into the calculator. While the calculator is processing this instruction, it sends back a disabling pulse (*busy*) that prevents further activity in the trigger generator. When the instruction has been completed, the busy pulse returns to its normal state and IC U generates a pulse. This pulse is fed to the word buffer count input, and the buffer is incremented to the next address. The execution of the instruction code in this new address is dependent on which key was depressed initially. If it was the R key, IC R is cleared and execution of all the remaining program instructions will take place until the generator sees an annunciator instruction code or the X key is depressed. After a pause or stop annunciator, which presents IC R, the program may be continued by pressing either key. If the X key had been depressed, the next instruction would not have been executed until either of the keys was pressed again, thus allowing the program to be executed step by step.

SEQUENCE GENERATOR

The four special instructions (GO TO, BR-, RET, and REM) are controlled by the sequence generator circuit shown in Fig. 8-14. When bit seven of the instruction code is activated, the sequence generator is enabled and the G2 input of the decoders is disabled.

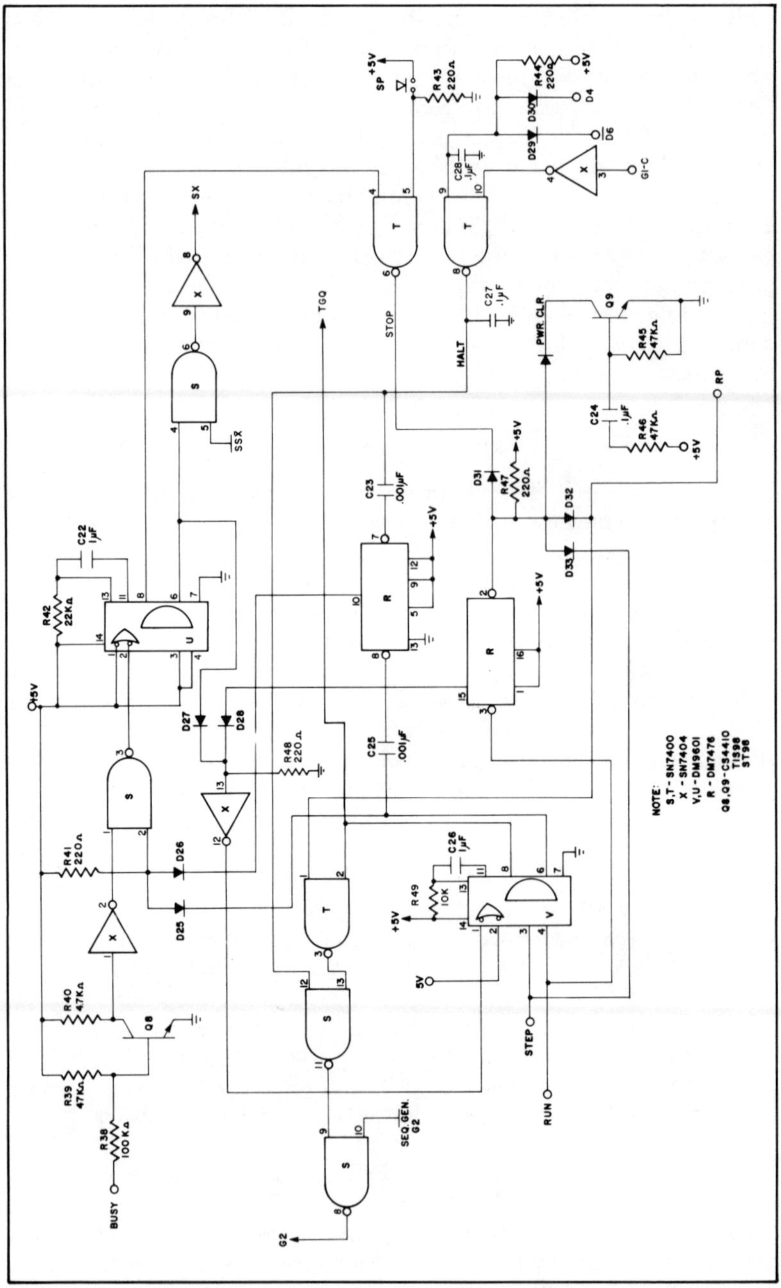

Fig. 8-13. MITS programmer trigger generator.

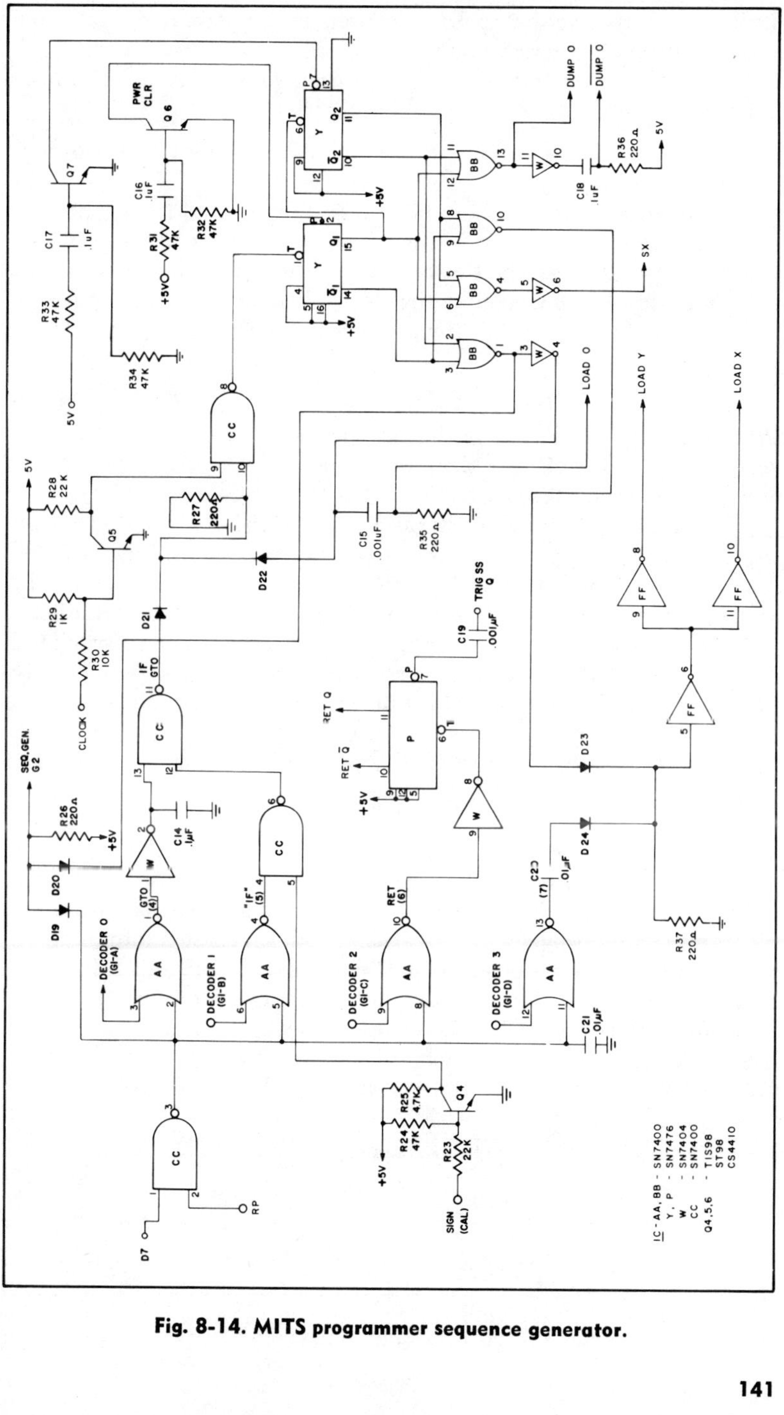

Fig. 8-14. MITS programmer sequence generator.

The special instruction to be executed is dependent on bits five and six of the instruction code.

When a GO TO command is seen by the programmer, the following sequence occurs:

1. The line address of the GO TO code (entered by the program used) is stored in the GO TO buffer.
2. The word buffer is incremented to the next address, and this new address is stored in the line and word return buffers.
3. The line address of the GO TO code is then entered into the line buffer and becomes the new address; the word buffer is cleared to zero so that the address is the first word of the new line.

The Branch if Minus (BR−) instruction operates in exactly the same way, but requires that a negative sign be present on the calculator display. If the display is positive, the command is ignored and passed over.

When a Return (RET) command is seen, the address stored by the branch instruction is loaded from the return buffers into the line and word buffers and becomes the new RAM address. This address is the one immediately following the branch instruction.

A Remember (REM) command has no initial branch associated with it. When the command is present, the address immediately following it is loaded into the line and word return buffers and continues to the next address for execution. The programmer can return to that address later in the program upon receiving a return command.

DISPLAY

The display, which is shown in Fig. 8-15, provides a visual indication of the programmer status. Each seven-segment digit is provided with a converter, which changes the incoming four-bit binary number into one of sixteen numbers or letters. The two left-hand digits indicate the current location addressed in the RAM page, with the left-most digit indicating the line address and the next digit to the right indicating the word address. The

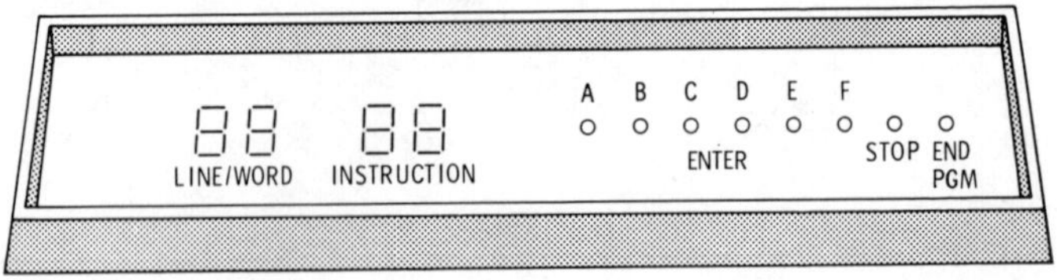

Fig. 8-15. MITS programmer display.

next two digits indicate the instruction code located in this address; the left digit represents the most significant digit, and the right digit indicates the least significant digit.

Eight LED indicator lights are adjacent to the four display readouts. The first six are marked A through F and indicate which variable should be entered into the calculator. The next light is labelled STOP and is used to stop the program to observe subtotals or to check correct execution. The END PGM (End of Program) should be the last instruction code in each program, signifying that execution of all program steps has been completed. Therefore, the END PGM annunciator light will be on at the end of a program.

OTHER PROGRAMMERS

This discussion of the operation of a typical programmer should provide some insight into the complexity of programmer design. As calculator prices stabilize at reasonable levels, more and more programmers will become commercially available. Added memory and increased power in even basic machines will greatly expand the capabilities of economical programmers such as those manufactured by MITS and other firms.

GLOSSARY OF TERMS USED WITH MITS PROGRAMMER

Address: A location in the RAM page that is capable of storing a seven-bit word. There are 256 addresses in each RAM page.

Annunciator Lights: A visual indication of the internal state of a program. A light appears on the display indicating the following:

- A through F—Execution is temporarily halted; the light identifies which variable is to be entered.
- STOP—Execution is halted so that the user can observe a subtotal (appearing on the calculator display) or check for a possible error in the program.
- END PGM—Execution is halted after the last step of a program; the light is used to separate programs.

Bit: The abbreviation for a binary digit; a minimal unit of information that is equal to one binary decision. It is always in one of two states (i.e., on/off or positive/negative).

Buffer: A temporary storage location for a four-bit binary number.

Increment: A term indicating an increase by one.

Instruction: A seven-bit word stored at a particular address. Two key depressions are required to enter an instruction into memory. The first is the most significant digit or MSD (the first four bits); the second is the least significant digit or LSD (the last three bits).

Line: A group of words (maximum of 16) used as a convenient way of addressing the RAM page.

Program: A group of instructions (simulating calculator key depressions or internal commands) required to perform a certain function. Each instruction is executed in the order it is entered.

RAM Page: A complete memory plane that can store two hundred fifty-six 7-bit words (16 lines × 16 words). In this programmer, seven RAMs comprise one RAM page.

Special Instruction: Internal commands which allow the user to program such subroutines as GO TO, BRANCH IF MINUS, RETURN, and REMEMBER.

Word: A group of seven bits occupying one memory location (seven bits are necessary to encode one instruction in this programmer).

MITS PROGRAMMER KEY AND SWITCH FUNCTIONS

PG1/PG2 Switch: This switch selects the memory page (always set to PG1 unless the programmer is an expanded version).

RUN/PGM *and* ADDR/INSTR *Switches:* These two switches work in conjunction with each other to determine programmer mode of operation.

0 through 9 and A through F keys: These keys have two functions: line address selection and program code entry.

R Key: This key causes the program to run in the continuous mode or increments the address in the address mode.

X Key: This key causes the program to run in the step mode or increments the address in the address mode.

S Key: This key halts the program execution. The R or X key must be pressed to restart the program. When this key is used, the program is stopped at a random step and the operator cannot be sure of stopping at a particular step.

Power Switch: When in the ON position, this switch activates the programmer. It should be left on when the unit contains programs, because turning it off clears all the data stored in the memory. There is a battery circuit that provides several hours of auxiliary power if the ac power to the unit fails.

CHAPTER 9

Servicing Electronic Calculators

Small electronic calculators require more sophisticated troubleshooting techniques than those employed in servicing many other kinds of electronic equipment. In addition to the basic procedures used in discrete transistor circuits, calculator servicing requires some understanding of integrated circuitry and logic.

To service a defective calculator you will need a pencil-type soldering iron (30 to 40 watts at about 700°F), small screwdrivers, solder remover, sharp knife, diagonal cutters, and needle-nose pliers. A vom and oscilloscope are the only necessary pieces of test equipment, but a frequency counter can come in handy at times. Some problems can be solved with no test equipment at all or possibly a vom alone.

BASIC TROUBLESHOOTING PROCEDURES

A few general procedures will save lots of time and reduce the chance of inadvertently damaging additional components in an already defective machine. First, give the machine a careful visual inspection. Burned or bubbly resistors, blown electrolytic capacitors, solder bridges, and other obvious malfunctions can usually be quickly found and corrected. If the problem involves a destroyed component, never install a replacement part until the cause of the problem is found and corrected. Never use a replacement component of less quality than the original one.

Next, although it may be necessary to turn on a calculator to find the symptoms of a problem, never leave a malfunctioning machine on longer than necessary. A good example is the overflow indicator. If the readout devices do not light, multiply two numbers whose product will give an overflow indication. If the "Error" signal is displayed, the problem is not in the input, control, or arithmetic sections of the machine. In this manner, possible causes of the trouble can be quickly identified.

Finally, if a thorough visual inspection fails to reveal the problem, begin troubleshooting at the point of the improper indication and work backward, checking each associated component. If more than one problem exists, begin with the simplest since it frequently leads to the major trouble spot. Here is a typical example:

In Fig. 9-1, the *C* segment in the display fails to light. Follow these steps to isolate the trouble:

1. Check continuity from the *C* segment to the Q5 emitter
2. Check the Q5 base for proper incoming signal
3. Check Q5
4. Check R15
5. Check R14

In order to cover as many troubleshooting procedures as possible, the remainder of this chapter will be divided into subsections describing the problems and symptoms common to the various subsections of almost all electronic calculators. The Trouble-

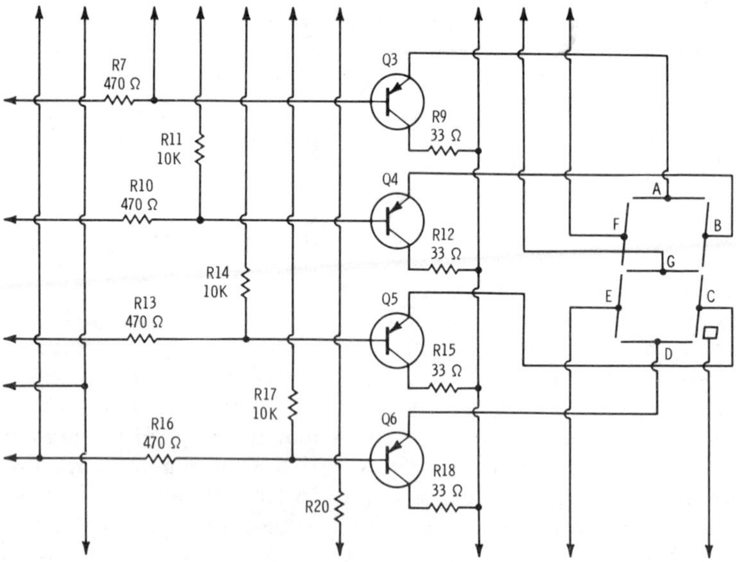

Fig. 9-1. Partial driver circuit for seven-segment readout.

shooting Chart at the end of this chapter summarizes this material and will help to pinpoint many trouble sources.

THE KEYBOARD

The keyboard consists of an array of switches either connected directly to the input LSI chip or encoded through a diode matrix. In the former technique the input chip automatically scans the keyboard to detect switch closures. In single-chip calculators, a similar process takes place.

In the latter technique, as shown in Fig. 9-2, the 0 through 9 digit keys are connected to a diode matrix which provides a BCD output. An open or shorted diode will cause incorrect segments on the display readouts to be illuminated. A shorted keyboard switch, either digit or function, can cause a great variety of symptoms.

After eliminating other possible causes of the problem, disconnect the keyboard and make entries manually by shorting the lines going to each switch. If this cures the problem, check each switch in the keyboard for continuity. If only one key fails to work properly, the problem is in the switch itself, an open line to the input section, or the input LSI chip. Another possible cause of trouble is input lines from the keyboard shorted to one another. This problem can be identified by using a vom to check for shorts.

In most multichip calculators and in newer single-chip machines, the input chip scans a keyboard matrix to detect entries. In Fig. 9-3, which shows the keyboard matrix for a MITS 816 desk calculator, the *X* lines are pulsed by the input chip and the Y lines

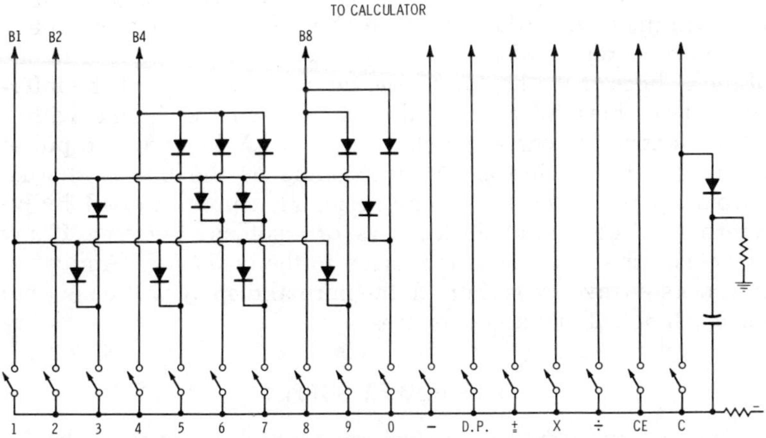

Fig. 9-2. Direct input diode-matrix keyboard.

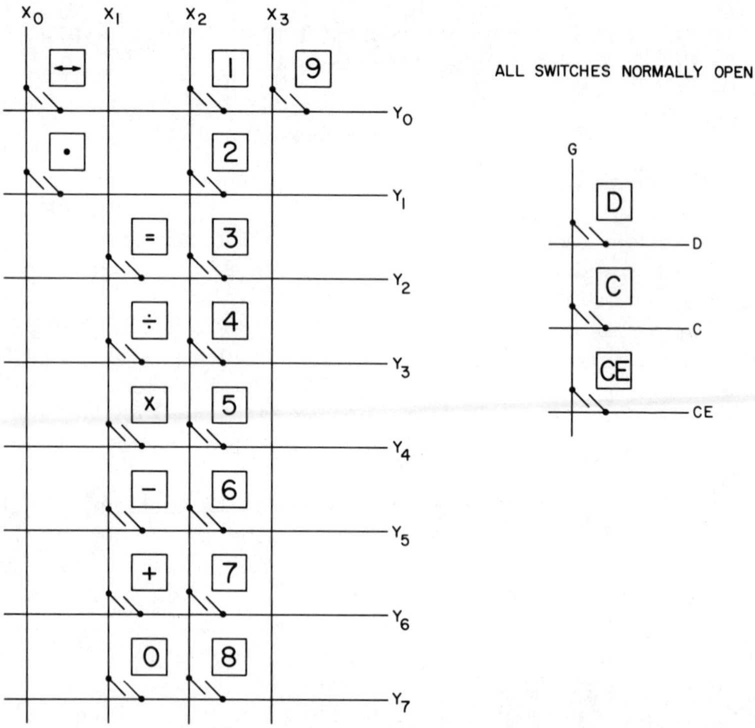

Fig. 9-3. Switch-matrix keyboard.

are at a negative voltage. When a key is depressed, there will be pulses on both lines common to the closed switch. The pulses can be seen on an oscilloscope; if they are not present, the problem is either in the keyboard or the input chip. If pulses are seen on a *Y* line with no keyboard entry, that particular line is shorted to one of the *X* lines at the keyboard, the input chip, or one of the interconnection lines. When no pulses appear on the *Y* line with a correct entry, the entry switch is open. An *X* line with no pulses means the input chip is not functioning or the line is shorted (probably to ground). A nonfunctioning chip is caused by an internal defect, lack of clock pulses, or insufficient voltage. If any key clears the machine, it is shorted to the CLEAR key. And when the CLEAR ENTRY key is shorted, the normal display will be on, but the machine will not accept entries.

THE POWER SUPPLY

Usually consisting of a transformer and one or more bridge rectifiers, some of which are regulated by either a transistor or a zener diode, the power supply is a major source of trouble in most electronic equipment. A close visual inspection is important when a malfunction points to the power supply. A shorted supply line, for example, will be indicated by a burned or bubbly series resistor and is usually caused by a shorted regulator, shorted filter capacitor, or possibly a short in the LSI circuitry.

The LSI chips sometimes require two regulated negative voltages, VGG and VDD. VGG is a higher voltage; if it is open or shorted, no entries will be possible and an error indication will sometimes be seen. With a missing VDD, there will be no display and no entries can be made.

If the driver voltage is shorted or open, the condition of the driver circuitry will determine whether the display readouts are all on or all off. But one of these malfunctions will be present.

Both gas-discharge and electrofluorescent readout devices require a large anode voltage, with the latter also requiring a filament voltage. The entire display will be off when either of these voltages is open or shorted. Figure 9-4 shows a typical power supply for a calculator that employs electrofluorescent readout devices. The +45 V is anode voltage and the −2.4 V is for the filaments. The −26 V and −14 V are VGG and VDD respectively, and the −5 V is the segment and digit-drive-bias voltage. If a bridge rectifier diode should short, the output voltage will be reduced. If an input filter capacitor should open, the readout tubes will receive unfiltered voltage and sometimes flicker on and off. If a capacitor shorts, its voltage line will be at zero potential and one or more bridge rectifier diodes may short.

Three of the lines shown in Fig. 9-4 use zener diodes for regulation. If the output is open, the total current in the line goes through the zener diode, sometimes causing it to short and the series resistor to bubble. The voltage line will read higher than normal if the zener opens. This may or may not cause a problem, and if the difference between the peak voltage and the rated voltage of the zener is only a few volts, the machine should operate normally.

THE CLOCK

LSI calculators, like full-scale digital computers, require a time base to synchronize all operations. The timing-pulse generator is called the *clock,* and it usually consists of an astable or free-running multivibrator or series of gates in a TTL chip. The former approach is used mainly in LSI calculators that require a two-phase clock. These are usually one- or two-chip machines. If the timing pulses are missing at the output of the clock IC, the problem is either in the chip or its associated components, or the supply voltage to the chip is open or shorted.

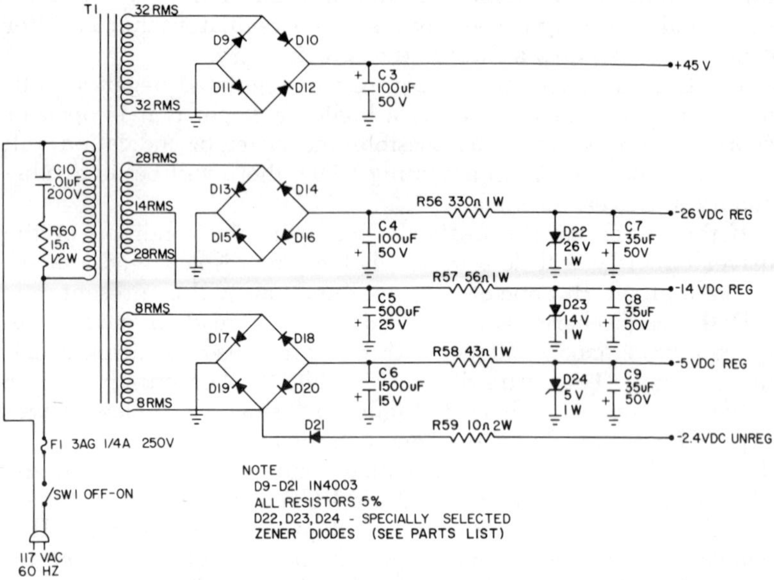

Fig. 9-4. MITS 816 calculator power supply.

Formerly most calculators required an external clock circuit. In recent years, however, many different calculator chips containing an integral clock have become available.

A representative TTL clock is shown in Fig. 9-5. The clock pulses are fed through a buffer for interfacing with the LSI chips, and the absence of pulses can frequently be traced to the buffer transistor. Check for proper voltage at both the transistor and the chip. If voltages are correct, check the clock chip in an IC tester or try it in another calculator. CAUTION: To avoid possible damage to the IC, never substitute a good chip for a bad one until the problem is discovered and eliminated.

DISPLAY DRIVERS

The driver system for a display consists of switching transistors which are sometimes arranged in a Darlington configuration for added current gain. At any one time, a driver transistor is either on or off. Driver circuits are required for the various digits and the segments within a digit, and both are described below.

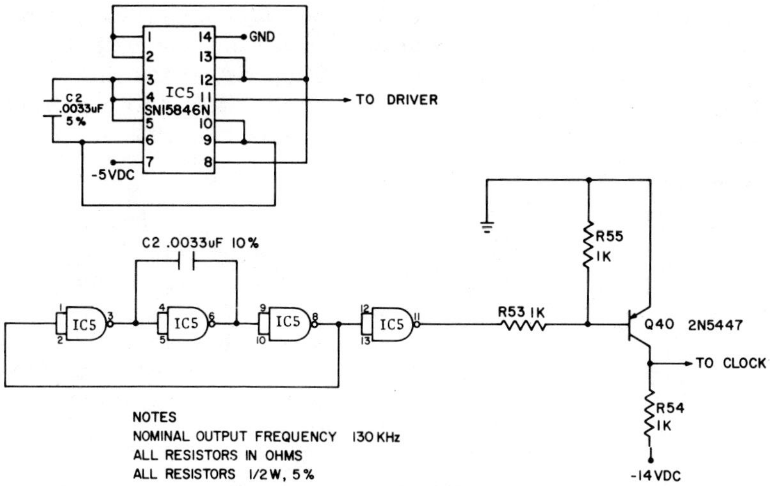

Fig. 9-5. Typical clock circuit.

Digit Drivers

The digit drivers are fed from the output LSI chip, and their output goes to the display device. Fig. 9-6 shows a typical switching configuration used in many drivers. Initially the base of Q15 will be positive with respect to its emitter and thus be driven into saturation. This pulls the Q16 base negative, turning off Q16 and the digit. When the proper command is received, the digit line output goes negative. This turns Q15 off, which forces Q16 into saturation, and the digit turns on.

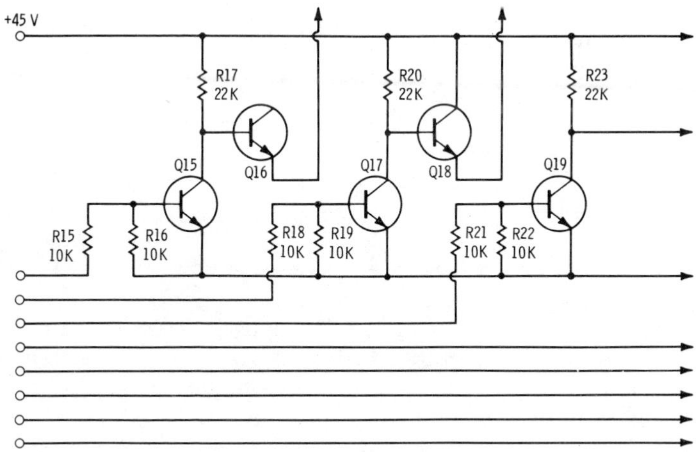

Fig. 9-6. MITS 816 digit drivers.

A digit which is constantly on can be caused by a faulty output LSI chip, an open interconnected lead from the chip to the driver, a condition of Q15 open or Q16 shorted, or the shorting of the readout anode to +V. Conversely, a digit that never turns on is caused by the opposite of any of the above problems.

Segment Drivers

The same basic circuit shown in Fig. 9-6 is used to drive the segments of the readout devices. The information coming from the output chip is fed through a bcd to a seven-segment converter, and then it is sent to the segment drivers.

In some driver circuits, such as the one shown in Fig. 9-7, a shorted transistor can cause the gate in the converter feeding the transistor to short. This is a good example of why a good IC should never be randomly substituted for a defective one. If at all possible, test the chip in another calculator or in an IC tester. If it is bad, find the cause of the problem before trying a new chip.

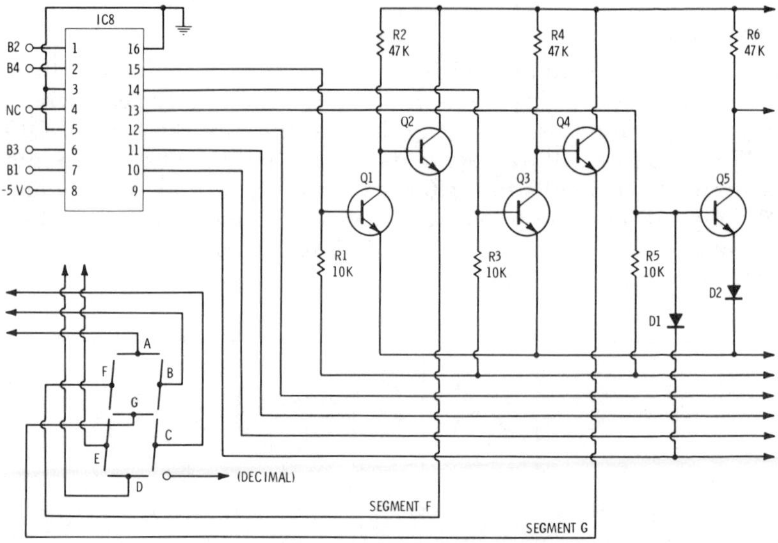

Fig. 9-7. BCD seven-segment decoder.

Operation of the driver in Fig. 9-7 is as follows: With no segments illuminated, the output bcd lines are at −5 V and the converter outputs are at 0 V. If a 2, for example, is entered on the keyboard, it will appear on the four bcd lines as: B1 = −5 V; B2 = 0 V; B3 = −5 V; and B4 = −5 V. This code at the input of the bcd converter will force the A, B, D, E, and G outputs to go to

−5 V and the remaining outputs will stay at 0 V. The −5 V signal at the Q1 base will cut off Q1, turn Q2 on, and cause the appropriate segment to be illuminated. This circuit is virtually identical to the digit driver discussed earlier, and the same service procedures apply.

DISPLAY DEVICES

As discussed in Chapters 5 and 6, most electronic calculators employ light emitting diode, gas-discharge, or electrofluorescent display devices. The LED readout has characteristics similar to those of a conventional diode. A typical seven-segment LED readout has 11 connection pins—1 per segment, 1 for the decimal point, and 3 for the anodes. LED readouts usually employ a series string of at least two diodes per segment to give dots which merge into a line pattren.

If all the diodes in a particular segment are not illuminated, the readout is defective and should be replaced. When the segments in an LED readout are shorted together internally, isolating the bad readout from others in the display may prove difficult. One way to find the bad readout is to measure the resistance between the two segments on each readout with a high-sensitivity ohmmeter, such as a bridge comparator. A second method is to remove each LED readout from the display and test it individually until the defective unit is located—a difficult procedure if the readouts are soldered in place. If a segment fails to light in only one readout, either the device or the solder joints at one or more of its pins are defective.

Gas-discharge and electrofluorescent readouts require far more driving voltage than LEDs. The light emitted by the gas-discharge device is a result of ionizing neon or some other gas by means of a moderately high voltage. Electrofluorescent devices employ an anode coated with a phosphor that produces light when struck by electrons. These units have a directly heated cathode and a control grid for acceleration that is usually at the same potential as the anode. A major problem in these readout tubes is the filament line. A shorted or open segment in either electrofluorescnt or gas-discharge readouts is very unlikely. If a problem should occur, the same procedures listed for troubleshooting LED displays apply.

AUTOMATIC CLEAR

When initially turned on, most calculators automatically reset to zero without the need for a command from the CLEAR key. A typical automatic clear circuit is shown in Fig. 9-8. In operation, the circuit momentarily grounds the clear line after power is applied to the machine. If the capacitor or resistor shorts, the indication is no display, and no entries are possible. A shorted diode will not affect the circuit each time the power is activated, but occasionally the machine will not automatically clear. An open capacitor or diode will disable the circuit, but the machine can be manually reset via the CLEAR key.

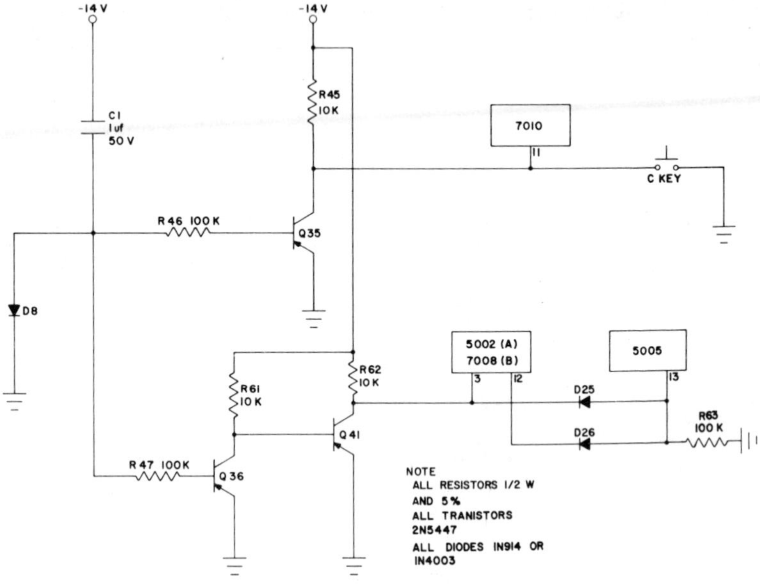

Fig. 9-8. Typical automatic clear circuit.

SIGN AND ERROR

The left-most readout on a display is generally used as a status indicator and receives only a few commands. The minus-sign indication and overflow signal come directly from an LSI chip through buffer stages. As shown in Fig. 9-9, there are only three components involved with these functions in a typical circuit. Troubleshooting procedures previously described also apply here.

CONSTANT FUNCTION

Many calculators have the ability to store a number in memory which can then be used to multiply or divide by any other numbers subsequently entered into the machine. This proce-

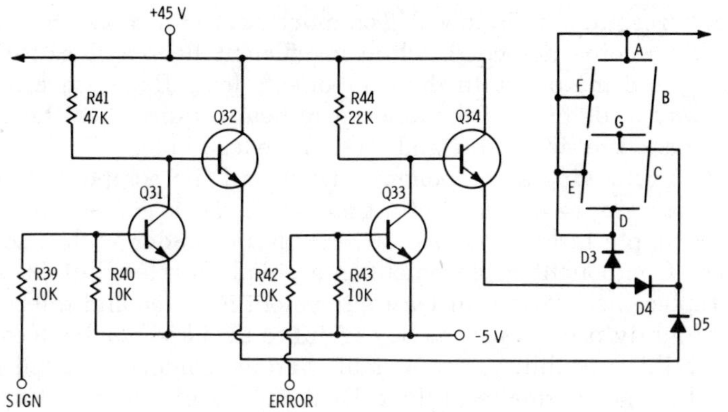

Fig. 9-9. Minus- and error-sign circuit.

dure is accomplished by means of a circuit such as the one in Fig. 9-10. In operation, Q36 is initially biased on, which keeps Q35 off. When the constant switch is turned on, Q36 is cut off by a positive voltage at its base, Q35 turns on, and pin 22 of the input chip is essentially placed at ground. This places the input chip in the constant mode. At the same time the large positive voltage lights the appropriate segments on the readout device to display a *C*. As with the sign and error function, the previous servicing techniques generally apply.

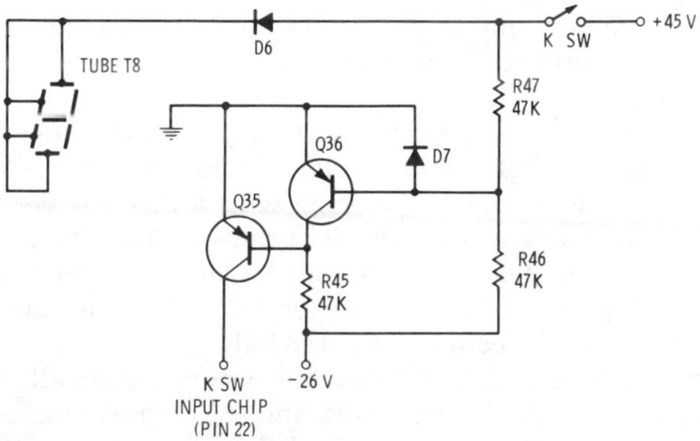

Fig. 9-10. Typical constant circuit (MITS 816).

CIRCUIT BOARDS AND SOLDERING

Supersmall calculators frequently require double-sided printed-circuit boards with plated-through holes. When a component is being removed from a plated-through hole, careful desoldering procedures must be followed. Too much heat will cause the metal land to become detached, while insufficient heat will cause the plating to come out with the components lead. Experience is the only way to determine the amount of heat required for the component and the size of the land around the lead hole.

When removing a component, always cut the component leads and then remove one lead at a time. Once the leads are removed it is a simple task to remove any remaining solder with a solder puller. Component replacement is a simple matter, but be sure the replacement part is at least equivalent in value and tolerance.

On tightly packed boards be careful to avoid solder bridges. To reduce this possibility, use a small-wattage soldering pencil iron and 24-gauge, or smaller, solder. Heat sinks are usually not necessary if solder time is limited to a few seconds and if care is taken to apply solder just after heat is applied. Metal lands that run very close together along the board are particularly susceptible to shorts caused by small, sometimes microscopic, slivers of metal. A magnifier and a sharp pointed probe are very helpful in removing such debris. A final tip concerning cold solder joints: When one is suspected, reheat the connection and add a small amount of new solder.

MOS LSI HANDLING PRECAUTIONS

So long as they are in the circuit, MOS LSI ICs are practically troublefree. When the chips are improperly handled, however, they become susceptible to damage from static electricity and mechanical pressure.

When removing a chip from a socket, ground the fingers on the calculator ground line (making sure the machine is not on) and pry up each side of the IC package with a screwdriver, using a gentle rocking motion until the IC comes loose. When the IC is free of the socket, pick it up without touching the pins and place the unit on a piece of Styrofoam covered with aluminum foil. All the pins should make contact with the foil.

When installing a chip in a socket, ground yourself and then carefully line up all the pins with the socket receptacles. Apply gentle pressure at first one end and then the other until the IC is secure in the socket.

> CAUTION: If the MOS LSI ICs are soldered in place, *do not* attempt removal unless the proper equipment and experience are available.

Troubleshooting the LSI portion of a calculator is extremely difficult if a block diagram showing inputs and outputs for each chip is not available. If the diagram is available, it can be used to work from the output chip or section of a chip backward to the input of the preceeding chip. This procedure is more difficult in multichip calculators since some chips invariably receive feedback input information from other chips.

CONCLUSION

This sums up many of the servicing problems encountered in troubleshooting electronic calculators on the market today. To see how the procedures are applied in a practical situation, refer to the following case histories.

The MITS 1440 is a high-quality multifunction desk calculator with a square and square-root capability. The machine can also store a 14-digit word in its memory and has a constant function. The unit incorporates 14 readouts in its display and six LSI chips. A machine came in for service in which the overflow indicator worked but the display failed to operate. The power-supply voltages and the pulses on the digit lines and BCD lines from the output chip to the display buffer were all good. Quoting from the servicing technician's report:

"I began looking at the input and output signals around the alternate display circuit (Fig. 9-11). I started at the outputs of the circuit (pins 4 and 10 of IC11), found they were not present, and began working backward until finding correct input pulses at pins 8 and 9 of gate 3A. There was no output at pin 10 of the IC socket. I then checked pin 10 at the IC lead and determined that it was operating properly. A continuity check showed an open between pin 10 of the socket and the IC. Resoldering the pin failed to correct the problem. I removed the socket and found that pin 10 had been broken internally. The socket was replaced, and when the chip was reinstalled, the machine operated properly."

The most time-consuming problems in multichip calculators are those associated with the metal lands on the circuit board, which interconnect the LSI chips. A malfunction of this type usually gives erratic symptoms that point to no particular trouble area. Each LSI chip has inputs, outputs, and feedback lines to the other chips which can make troubleshooting quite difficult and time-consuming. Fig. 9-12 shows the interconnection pattern for the four chips of the MITS 816. The interconnections require so many crossovers that a double-sided circuit board is required. This, of course, further complicates location of open or shorted lands.

Excerpts from the servicing technician's troubleshooting report illustrate two typical circuit-board problems. Both involve the MITS 816.

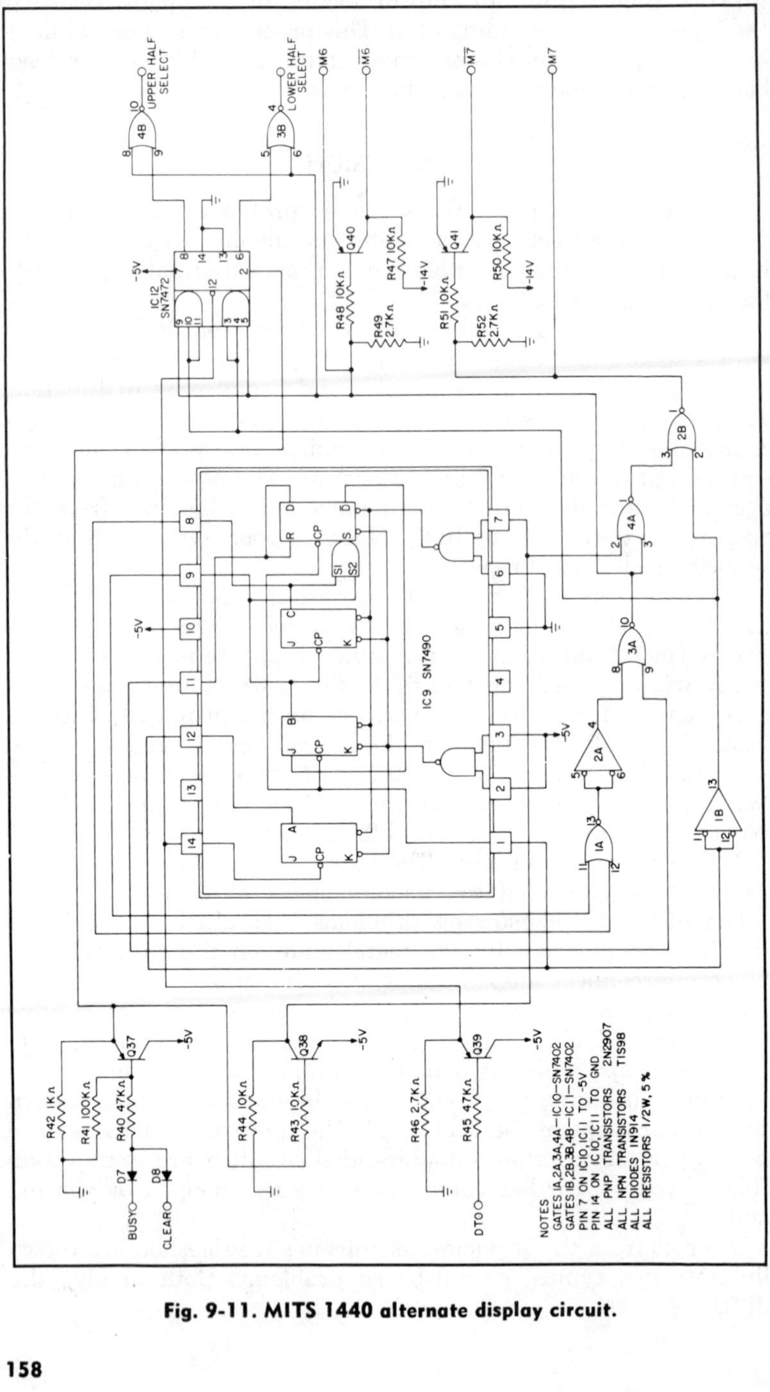

Fig. 9-11. MITS 1440 alternate display circuit.

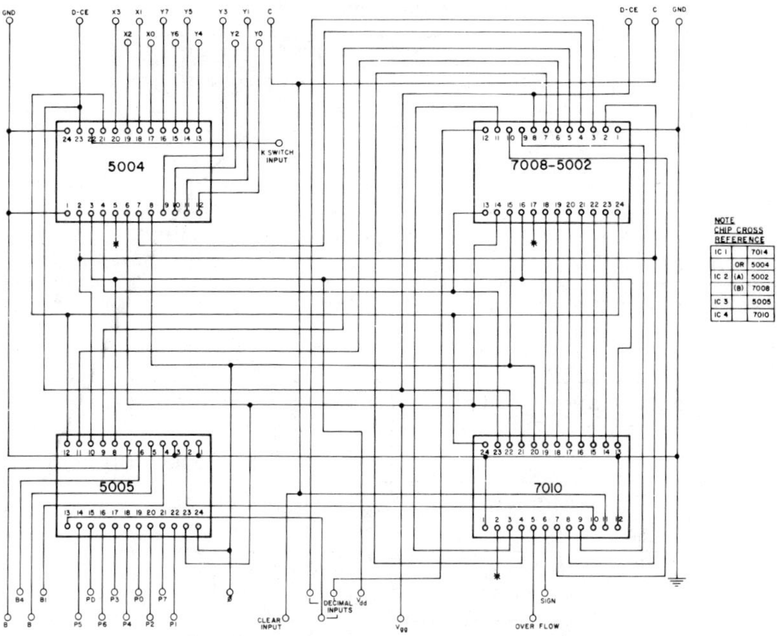

Fig. 9-12. MITS 816 chip interconnections.

1. "The machine generated a random number sequence on the display. Power-supply voltages, keyboard lines, and the ICs were all good. I began looking at the signals entering and leaving each LSI chip and comparing them with similar signals in a good machine.

   The voltage level on pin 10 of IC-7010 did not change as it did on the good unit. I checked continuity from pin 10 to all the metal lands on the circuit board than ran along the land connecting pin 10 to pin 2 of IC-5005 and discovered a short between that land and the data line (pin 24, IC-7010; pin 12, IC-5005; etc.). With a magnifying glass I located a tiny sliver of metal bridging the two lands together. Removal of the sliver corrected the malfunction."
2. "The machine produced a normal on condition, but no entries were possible. Past experience helped greatly with this particular problem. I checked the power supply and input chip, and both were good.

   One input line to the input IC, the "busy" line, disables this chip while the machine is performing calculations. When this line is active (at −14 V dc), the machine will not accept entries. Therefore, I checked continuity between the busy

Chart 9-1. Troubleshooting Chart

SYMPTOM	*TROUBLESHOOTING PROCEDURE*
No display or entry	Check: Power supply Clear circuit Clock circuit
Overflow works but no display	Check: Power supply LSI chips (output)
Display always on or off	Check: Display digit driver Soldering LSI chips (output)
Segment always on or off	Check: Segment drivers Soldering LSI chips (output)
More than one segment or display device on	Check: Soldering
Keyboard switch failure	Check: Keyboard LSI chips (input)
All digits on or off	Check: Power supply
Random segments on	Check: LSI chips (output) Segment drivers
Function key failure	Check: LSI chips (arithmetic)
Entries not possible (display normal)	Check: Keyboard LSI chips
Constant function always on	Check: Constant circuit and switch LSI chips (input)
Display warms up and turns off	Check: Soldering LSI
Display flickers	Check: Power supply
Error indicator on and no entries possible	Check: Power supply

line and the −14 V line and found, as suspected, a short between the two lines. Following these lines I eventually found a small solder bridge under the circuit board which occurred during the wave-soldering operation. After the short was removed, the unit operated correctly."

The case study just cited is one of the few associated with the LSI chips which can be performed in a logical, step-by-step manner. Other problems which appear to involve the chip or chips require careful inspection of the circuit board and solder connections. If no obvious trouble is located, a chip may be defective.

There are numerous other examples of calculator troubleshooting. The best way to learn the techniques is to gain experience by servicing actual machines. The troubleshooting chart in Chart 9-1 can serve as a general guideline.

CHAPTER 10

Calculators Today and Tomorrow

Calculator technology has made significant advances since the first multiple-IC units were introduced several years ago. Improvements in MOS LSI have resulted in single chips capable of the four standard arithmetic operations as well as square root and memory. Single-chip machines are much more compact than their multiple-chip predecessors.

Advances in chip design, keyboards, displays, driving techniques, and packaging have combined to make for a generation of calculators that obsoletes many units manufactured more than a few years ago. In this concluding chapter, we'll look at some of the advances in calculator design, consider the relative merits of various machines, and make a few predictions.

CALCULATORS TODAY

A recent issue of *Government Product News,* a trade publication that includes descriptions of office equipment, listed more than 350 calculators made by companies in the United States and abroad. The calculator market changes so fast that some of the machines were obsolete by the time they were listed in GPN, others are no longer being manufactured, and many new machines have been added. Of equal significance, the original price for many of the machines has dropped, some significantly.

Calculators available today can be listed in three basic categories: Nonprogrammable machines with display, nonprogrammable machines with printer, and programmable machines. Of course, numerous variations of these basic categories are possible. The Hewlett-Packard HP-9820, a programmable calculator, is available with both printer and display as well as a variety of other useful options.

One of the most compact calculators available is made by Sinclair Radionics Ltd. of Great Britain and weighs only 2.5 ounces with its three miniature 1.3-volt mercury cells in place. The calculator measures only 5.5 by 2.25 by 0.375 inches and achieves a remarkably low average power consumption of only about 30 mW in a novel manner. Instead of being operated continuously as in a conventional machine, the Texas Instruments MOS chip used in the calculator is pulsed at a rate of 200 kHz by 1.7-microsecond trigger pulses. Since the only pulsing occurs when the chip is actually working, a considerable power savings over conventional machines ensues.

One of the cheapest mass-production calculators available is made by Litronix. This machine has an eight-digit, floating point readout, and four functions. Even cheaper calculators will be available in coming years.

Another economical calculator is the Sharp ELSI MATE EL-120. The EL-1230 uses bright, attractive electrofluorescent display tubes. Full twelve-digit capability is retained in the LSI chip, which is the heart of the machine. To read out all digits of a solution having more than three digits, the user can command the display through a step sequence. The calculator includes a capability for automatic sequencing of a result as well.

A unique feature of the EL-120 is a *count* button. The user can press the COUNT key to record various events—and even perform calculations on the result. Conventional calculators also count, but a few keyboard manipulations are required.

Operating from three easily obtained alkaline penlight cells, the EL-120 has a battery life of 15 hours. The machine consumes 600 milliwatts in operation. The three-digit output of the EL-120 is inconvenient for many applications, but the cost savings has attracted many customers.

Inexpensive four-function machines represent only one area of development, and there is a major trend toward development of economical multiple-function and scientific calculators. The MITS 941 Metric Converter and 7440 Scientific Calculator are just two examples of these more sophisticated machines. The 941 was shown in Fig. 1-14, and the 7440 is shown in Fig. 10-1. The 7440 has complete algebraic entry and keyboard functions such as e^x, reciprocal, square root, pi, x^y, $\log_{10}{}^x$, memory, and the trigonometric functions. The 7440 costs less than the four-function machines did a few years ago, and, when paired with a MITS programmer, the 7440 has many of the capabilities of a minicomputer.

The calculators described above represent only a small sampling of the literally hundreds of units that are commercially available. Besides these relatively low-cost machines, there are more advanced calculators. Two advanced programmable units made by Hewlett-Packard are representative of this class of machines.

HP-9820

The distinction between programmable calculators and minicomputers becomes fuzzy with a consideration of Hewlett-Packard's HP-9820 programmable desktop calculator (Fig. 1-17).

Fig. 10-1. The MITS 7440 advanced scientific calculator.

This remarkable machine provides the capability of a minicomputer. The most significant difference between the former and the latter is the 9820 entry system. The five banks of keyboards permit equations to be entered into the machine, and a START key is pressed to initiate the calculation sequence. The solution is displayed on a 16-character light emitting diode display, a paper tape, or an X-Y plotter. The LED display also displays the symbols, characters, and digits as they are entered into the machine.

Like its predecessor, the 9810, the 9820 can be programmed to solve complex simultaneous equations. The basic machine comes with 173 registers, but can be expanded to 429 registers with plug-in cartridges. The fully expanded machine can solve up to 36 simultaneous equations having as many as 36 unknowns.

The 9820 incorporates features that greatly simplify problem solving and programming. For example, if a language error is entered, an error notice flashes on the display so corrective action can be taken. At the push of a key, all entries can be printed out for proofreading. If errors are found or if changes are to be made, entire lines of data or instruction can be easily erased from the machine memory.

The 9820 provides almost infinite user flexibility by incorporating three banks of custom keyboards. Cartridges of read-only memory available from Hewlett-Packard can be plugged into the machine and templates placed over the keys to greatly expand the basic machine. The ROM cartridges include various mathematical functions, instructions for auxiliary equipment, and custom memories that can be defined by the user.

HP-9830

Hewlett-Packard's latest addition to its line of programmable desktop calculators is the 9830. This machine completes the transition from advanced calculators to true minicomputers by employing *Basic,* an advanced computer language. Like the 9820, the 9830 employs a complete alphanumeric keyboard. Entered data, statements, equations, etc., are displayed on a 32-character light emitting diode display. An accessory thermal printer, which silently produces page-width hard copy at eighty characters per line and 250 lines per minute (or 330 characters per second), is available.

Since the 9830 utilizes Basic, the machine can be coupled to a computer that also uses Basic for expanded memory capability. Even on its own, however, the 9830 incorporates an ample 40-kilobyte memory with optional ROM modules available for special purpose and user-definable functions.

Operation of the 9830 is enhanced by a self-contained cassette-tape memory. Each cassette contains an 80-kilobyte memory and can store programs, instructions, and data, in any format the user selects. The cassette system provides both read-only and read-write capabilities. An automatic search mechanism seeks out instructions or data called out by the operator. An interrupt capability halts the search procedure to permit operation of the calculator whenever desired.

Desktop calculators have not reached their pinnacle in the remarkably advanced 9830. Despite the exceptional versatility and power of this machine, advances in miniaturization and memory technology will almost certainly reduce the size and further increase the capability of future 9830s.

Mathematics is not the exclusive domain of memories, of course, and the capability of advanced programmable machines to store programs and data entries hints at futuristic applications unheard of a few years ago.

CHOOSING A CALCULATOR

Choosing an electronic calculator can be a trying experience. Since technological improvements are still entering the commercial marketplace, a calculator can be made technologically obsolete overnight. But technological obsolescence, as aptly demonstrated by the abacus, does not detract from the usefulness of a machine. For this reason, do not ignore a machine which is not as advanced as newer models if it provides the arithmetic and operational functions you require, particularly since a price savings might be available over newer, more complex machines.

KITS VERSUS ASSEMBLED MACHINES

MITS, Inc. introduced the first kit calculator in 1971, and the firm now offers a variety of handheld and desktop kit and assembled machines. The Heath Company also offers calculator kits.

Kit calculators can be built in a reasonable amount of time at a respectable cost savings over assembled units. Besides saving money, assembly of a kit provides an interesting diversion and is an educational experience in itself. The latter point coupled with the excellent instruction manuals provided by large calculator kit companies like MITS and Heath makes troubleshooting a defective calculator feasible.

CALCULATORS VERSUS MINICOMPUTERS

With the immense problem-solving ability of today's programmable calculators, the capabilities of calculators and minicomputers begin to merge. The result can be a difficult decision for an individual, school, or company requiring more calculating power than that offered by a rather basic scientific machine.

When evaluating the relative merits and demerits of programmable calculators versus minicomputers, remember that calculators are designed for convenient problem solving, while computers are capable of far more applications. While a computer can do anything a calculator can, a calculator cannot handle the vast range of data-processing chores for which computers are ideal.

Thus far, the computer comes out ahead in overall capability, but frequently the vast capability of a computer is not required for most or even all of the calculating requirements found in many offices and laboratories. It is these more limited calculating roles that are ideally suited for a calculator.

Unlike the computer, access to a programmable calculator is virtually instantaneous. Memory capability and operating time are inferior to computers, but calculators can be addressed by means of a simple keyboard input. Computers require a program to solve even the simplest problems. Programs are lists of specific instructions or statements written in one of several computer languages which order the computer through the various steps required to solve a problem. Programmable calculators can also be programmed, but their read-only memory contains numerous prerecorded program steps that greatly simplify the operation of a calculator over that of a computer. For example, the self-contained programs of a programmable calculator include such provisions as error detection and indication. If an incorrect or incomplete entry is made into the machine, the display flashes an error signal. Some machines have a stored program that analyzes the error and displays a coded symbol telling the operator exactly what needs to be corrected. While all this capability is built into a calculator, it must be programmed into a computer.

A major advantage of calculators over computers is accessibility. Due to the cost of procuring and operating most computer systems, users must usually go through an administrative procedure to gain even limited access to the machine. Programs must be run and checked for errors, a procedure which may take several cycles and require repeated visits to the computer or terminal.

Calculator access is much faster and far more convenient. Problems requiring a program can be checked and edited right on the machine in a matter of minutes. The flexibility of a keyboard containing numerous complex functions is a big time-saver.

Still another calculator-computer consideration is the availability of interfaces and auxiliary equipment. The fact that computers have been around far longer than programmable calculators has automatically granted computer peripheral equipment a big lead over calculator peripherals. Appropriate computer peripherals permit complex interfacing between other systems and computers, a process not yet possible with calculators.

Nevertheless, several classes of very useful calculator peripherals are available. Printers, plotters, card and tape readers, supplemental memories, and user-definable keyboards are just some of them.

There are many applications where the power, speed, and versatility of a computer is an absolute requirement. For applications which emphasize calculating and require convenience and simple operating procedures, the programmable calculator is the best choice. The calculator provides the added benefits of relative portability, availability of economical peripherals, and an incentive to solve problems which previously went unsolved due to the time required to program them into a computer.

CALCULATORS TOMORROW

Making technological predictions is a risky business. The present widespread utilization of LSI in such consumer products as handheld calculators and watches would not have been expected a few years ago because of the primitive nature of integrated circuitry. Similarly, it is difficult to predict what developments may occur over the next ten years that will make electronic calculators even more sophisticated than those available today.

Nevertheless, we can safely make a few specific predictions and then hazard a guess at a few less certain, more exotic possibilities. On the safe side, it is certain that calculator prices will continue to plummet. As this is written, several firms are selling four-function machines with a $29.50 retail price. These machines usually have less readout digits than their more costly counterparts, some have no decimal indication, and they are therefore of limited usefulness. Nevertheless, housewives and students requiring only limited capability can effectively utilize an inexpensive, three- or six-digit machine.

Even machines employing the conventional eight or more digit displays will most certainly become less expensive as production and competition increase while costs for the expensive calculator chips and display elements decrease. Price reductions and improved chips will make possible economical multifunction machines with such additional capabilities as square root, square, memory, percentage, and others. These new calculators will sell for about the same price of simple four-function machines now so popular.

While there will also be a market for very inexpensive calculators, many customers prefer more quality and capability and are willing to pay for these added features. Therefore, calculator manufacturers will continue to introduce multiple-function machines having capabilities far beyond those of basic four-function units and costing somewhat more.

Besides increased complexity at reduced cost, calculator size will continue to be reduced. Pocket machines will become much thinner as keyboards are miniaturized and battery size is reduced. Battery size will be reduced as a direct result of NMOS and

CMOS LSI in place of the presently used PMOS LSI. Liquid-crystal displays will be commonplace, and their compact dimensions and very low power drain will make important contributions to calculator miniaturization.

If past and present trends are a proper indication, the ultimate limiting factors for calculator miniaturization is the size of the keyboard and display. Keyboards cannot be made much smaller than they are now because the size of the human finger requires a finite separation between individual keys. Similarly, displays must be large enough for legible reading. The obvious conclusion is that miniaturization will result in thinner rather than significantly smaller machines.

ELECTRONIC DICTIONARIES

No substantial advances in the state of conventional MOS memory technology are needed to produce advanced semiconductor memory systems. David Hodges, associate professor of electrical engineering at the University of California and a memory consultant, has predicted that a 50-megabit memory occupying only one cubic foot could be built by 1980 using technology available in 1973. Hodges' memory would have a density of 30,000 bits per cubic inch, a power consumption of 100 watts, and a cost of $20,000. While the price tag appears high, it's only 0.04 cents per bit.

Memory capabilities such as these leads to fascinating speculations concerning evolution of the calculator.

When and if multimegabit memories become available in a practical configuration and for a reasonable price, the role of the calculator will be greatly expanded. For example, it will be possible to use a pocket-sized machine as a combination telephone directory, diary, notebook, appointment calendar, and dictionary. Frequently used formulas, equations, hard to spell words, phone numbers, addresses, business contacts, *ad infinitum,* could be stored in the machine memory simply by keying in the appropriate data. Readout could be achieved by a paper tape which would rapidly and silently print the requested information when an encoded instruction was keyed into the machine.

All this may sound hard to believe but so was the existence of pocket-sized electronic slide rules only five years ago. MOS LSI and memory technology are advancing steadily, and it is quite possible that an electronic scratch pad will become a practical reality in the next few years.

Index

D

K

L

M

N

T

U

V

W

X

Z